THE
LAST
VICTIM

THE LAST VICTIM

TRACY HALL

WITH SUMMER LAND

hachette
AUSTRALIA

Published in Australia and New Zealand in 2024
by Hachette Australia
(an imprint of Hachette Australia Pty Limited)
Gadigal Country, Level 17, 207 Kent Street, Sydney, NSW 2000
www.hachette.com.au

Hachette Australia acknowledges and pays our respects to the past, present and
future Traditional Owners and Custodians of Country throughout Australia
and recognises the continuation of cultural, spiritual and educational practices
of Aboriginal and Torres Strait Islander peoples. Our head office is located on
the lands of the Gadigal people of the Eora Nation.

A catalogue record for this
book is available from the
National Library of Australia

ISBN: 978 0 7336 5115 1 (paperback)

Cover design by Luke Causby
Front cover and internal picture section photographs from the author's collection unless
otherwise credited
Tracy Hall's author photograph by Jaala Alex
Summer Land's author photograph by Amber Hooper
Typeset in Sabon LT Std by Kirby Jones
Printed and bound in Australia by McPherson's Printing Group

The paper this book is printed on is certified against the
Forest Stewardship Council® Standards. McPherson's Printing
Group holds FSC® chain of custody certification SA-COC-005379.
FSC® promotes environmentally responsible, socially beneficial
and economically viable management of the world's forests.

FOR MY DAUGHTER ASHA
who provided me with hope and life
when I needed it most

CONTENTS

Who the F***
is Hamish?

There are many mornings where I've had to jumpstart my body with caffeine before I can even think about being a contributing member of society. However, I can confidently say that Tuesday, 11 July 2017, was not one of them. My alarm buzzed at 6 am like usual. Typically a gratuitous snoozer, I uncharacteristically sprung out of bed like a gazelle who'd just been told she can live happily ever after in a predator-free plain with endless grass to munch on. Why the sudden elation, energy and sense of ease? For the first time in what felt like years, I woke up feeling fulfilled in every life area. Family – tick, career – tick, personal growth – tick, health – tick, relationship – double tick. Could this be the elusive 'contentment' I'd heard so many speak of?

After I pulled on a hoodie, I walked into my lounge room, cranked up the heater and opened the blinds. Even though the sun wouldn't rise for another hour, I like to passively people-watch the early morning walkers, runners, surfers and cafe coffee drinkers as they make their way to Freshwater Beach. If it had been one of my rare kid-free days, I would have joined them. Instead, I made a cup of tea and sat at my kitchen bench to double-check the morning's itinerary. It was school holidays so I was on duty to drive my seven-year-old daughter, Asha, and my friend's two kids to gymnastics camp before heading to work at eBay's Sydney office. When I picked up my phone to let my friend know my ETA, I saw a text from a name that still managed to make my stomach flip after almost eighteen months of dating: Max.

Max: Work work work xx

He sent the message at 1.37 am. *Odd.* For how much freedom Max had as a Bondi-based investment executive, one of the downsides was needing to action trades when the New York and/or London and/or Japanese stock exchanges were open. Thankfully, both of us had managed to avoid all work during our escape to Byron Bay that we'd recently returned home from. This little pocket of paradise had become such a frequent holiday destination that we'd actually met with a real estate agent to inspect a cottage on our most recent trip. Often used as the backdrop in influencer #notsponsored posts and major fashion campaigns, it was fully renovated, a five-minute walk from both Main and Tallow beaches and had the type of interior that would make Miranda Kerr's interior designer weep with envy. Basically, it was what $3 million beach home dreams were made of, and exactly where I imagined hosting family on holidays and friends seeking refuge from the Sydney rat race.

Before I had the chance to text back a few words of sympathy for his late-night work session, I heard Asha's feet making their way down her bunk bed ladder and into the kitchen. It was officially time to clock on. In the flurry of chaos that we like to call our morning routine, Asha ate her standard breakfast of Weet-Bix and Vegemite toast, while I searched high and low for not *a* leotard but *the* leotard, had a brief argument about a bump in her hair that I honestly couldn't see, filled up water bottles, packed lunches and managed to squeeze in a chat with our neighbour before hopping in the car. Fifteen minutes later, I pulled into my friend's driveway and noticed I had missed a call from Max.

Assuming he needed to debrief after a doozy of a work night, I flicked him a quick text.

Tracy: Oh babe, what happened? I'm just picking up three kids. Will call later x.

Within seconds, I had not one but three seven-year-olds to serve and was quickly discovering just how many renditions of 'Despacito' could happen at the same time inside an unassuming VW Golf. Once I unloaded the kids into the hands of gymnastics instructors (who absolutely deserve medals both on and off the mat), I took advantage of the soothing silence that made up the rest of my commute. Work would be every bit as overstimulating, so it was crucial to get into the right mindset before walking through my office doors.

As suspected, I was under the pump all day going from meeting to meeting, followed by agency presentations, emails, phone calls and staff one-on-ones. I don't think I even had time to go to the toilet. At some point, I sought sustenance from an expired protein bar in my top drawer but other than that, it was go, go, go! My first chance to think about anything other than marketing campaigns and deadlines came when I'd zipped up my work bag and headed to grab my car from the parking station. I shot a quick text to my friend letting her know I'd get Asha at 7 pm before ringing Max. No answer. He also hadn't responded to my earlier text so I quickly sent another before getting in my car.

Tracy: You ok, babe? Worried about you. x

My evening commute is one of my most sacred times. Unlike in the mornings when I'm visualising important conversations, workshopping solutions to problems or just transitioning from mum to marketing executive, I like to spend the drive home catching up on my personal life. Depending on my energy levels, I'll call friends and family for a good chinwag or decompress by listening to a podcast. On this particular drive, I was swapping between *Triple J Hack*, *The Squiz* and my internal soundtrack of anxious thoughts about why Max wasn't answering my calls or texts. *Did the Byron Bay house inspection give him cold feet? Was my enthusiasm too much? Or is he still getting slammed with work?*

That evening while Asha was having a shower and

getting ready for me to read to her in bed, I tried ringing Max again to no avail. At 8.14 pm, I sent another text.

Tracy: Please tell me you're ok.

I know my multiple calls and texts may be screaming 'Stage 5 Clinger' right now, but here's the thing: Max was a creature of habit. Aside from the odd middle-of-the-night trading demand, he was always fast asleep by 9 pm and sipping a ristretto by 4 am. Yes, his coffee choice is as pretentious as it sounds and one I admit I had to google to understand, but I digress ... Next, he'd either go for a run or surf, only returning once the sun was high in the sky and its warmth deep within his skin. From there, it was time to check the markets in Australia, Asia, the US and Europe via the bank of monitors in his home office. The reason I knew this was because Max usually gave me a play-by-play of his actions (as well as pithy commentary on the ongoings of international finance affairs) via text and photos each day. Seeing as I hadn't heard any predictions about France's new president, clearly something was wrong.

Instead of blissfully dreaming about beach homes, I spent the entire night worrying that Max had gotten hurt or died in a surfing or car accident. Thinking a shark or Bondi Beach death would certainly be newsworthy, I frantically began searching online:

Max Tavita Shark Attack
Bondi Beach Shark Attack
Surfer Death Bondi Beach

Max Tavita Surfing Accident
Shark Sighting Bondi Beach

Zero hits. I placed my phone back on my bedside table and wondered who Max had as his emergency contact. It hadn't occurred to me to update mine from my family to him so I doubt he'd listed me. That night, there were microsleeps here and there, but by 5.17 am I was beside myself with worry. I sent one final text pleading for him to respond.

> Tracy: I'm so worried hon, I don't have anyone's phone numbers to check you're ok. Please just text back or call and let me know you're ok.

With my lounge room shades still closed, I opened my laptop and started searching for anyone I thought might know something about Max. First, I tried to find his brother-in-law Chris on LinkedIn. I didn't see him there but remembered he was a sports coach in Canberra. Feeling desperate, I contacted the number listed on the website and left a message. While waiting for a reply, I started looking for a guy on Facebook that Max told me he surfed with most mornings. I didn't know his surname, but how many people named Sage could there be in Bondi? (Now that I think about it, probably a lot!) I knew my desperation was really peaking when I googled the name of the company that Max's childhood foster family owned. Anything. I was clutching on to anything.

As images of Max's body washing up on a beach continued to dramatically flash in my mind, I called Bondi

Police and asked if they could do a wellness check. The officer on the phone asked me about Max's mental state. No, he didn't have a history of mental illness, and no, he didn't seem like he could be a danger to himself ... it was just *so unlike him* to not be in contact. The officer asked if I could go and check on him. Already feeling stretched thin, I explained my situation – Northern Beaches single mum with a full-time job in the CBD to get to. Sympathetic, the officer said someone from Bondi Police would go check and call me back. Just as I was thanking them, Asha appeared in the kitchen which reminded me that I needed to do gymnastics carpooling before heading to work again. With virtually no sleep, I used pure adrenaline to replicate yesterday's morning routine of whipping up breakfast, packing lunches and ensuring I didn't *ruin* Asha's life by suggesting she wear *a* and not *the* leotard.

In the process of becoming the packhorse I need to be to get out the door, my phone started ringing. Hoping it was Max, I figuratively dropped everything as well as literally my work bag, car keys and Asha's gym bag in an effort to answer it. It wasn't Max but it was someone I was relieved to hear from. Without saying a proper hello, I found myself panic-telling my friend Cath that I hadn't heard from Max in over twenty-four hours and was worried that he had died or hit his head while out surfing. When I finally gave Cath the opportunity to speak, she calmly said, 'Trace, I'm going to send you a link to a news article and then I want you to call me back straight away.'

Instantly, my hands were shaking and I felt dizzy. *He's dead, he's dead, he's dead*, swirled in my head. I checked to see that Asha was in her room before clicking on the link. Within seconds, I was watching a video of an unidentified man being arrested outside an apartment I knew very well. The media did their best to blur his identity, but there was no hiding the fact that this man was, without a doubt, Max Tavita.

'Oh fuck, oh fuck, oh fuck,' seemed to be the only words I could mutter when I got back on the phone with Cath. Okay, so Max wasn't dead. He was arrested. *But why?*

Cath, a woman who could no doubt run the world, told me she was looking into it and would call me back as soon as she knew more. As my eyes tried to compute the images of Max being led to a police car, I could feel my chest tightening, my stomach twisting and my brain entering overdrive. Pretty quickly, I concluded that no amount of mindfulness could stop the tidal wave of shock, fear and pain from washing over me. Even though I could have earned an Oscar for my performance of the Calm and Happy Mum while doing the gymnastics run, these feelings got heavier and heavier on my drive into the city. With work being the last thing on my mind, I called anyone and everyone I could think of to learn more about Max. It was only when I called the Bondi Police to say they no longer needed to do a wellness check on Max because he'd been arrested that the weight of my feelings nearly broke me.

Right before I hung up, the officer stopped me. 'Just so you know, the name of the person you gave us – as well as his DOB – doesn't match the person who lives there.'

My mind instantly replayed the video of the man being escorted in handcuffs. Hair like Khaleesi from *Game of*

Thrones, eyes like a Disney prince and skin like a *Real Housewives* cast member ... it was definitely Max.

Baffled, I asked, 'What's his name?'

'Unfortunately, I can't tell you. You'll need to speak to a detective from Manly Police. They're leading the investigation.'

Struggling for words, I thanked the officer for their help and hung up. When I parked my car, I became paralysed by the endless stream of questions racing through my mind. *What's Max's real name? Why was he arrested? What could he have possibly done? Why was Manly Police investigating him? Was this something to do with his investments? Surely this is a mistake?* And then a question came that caused me to nearly keel over: *What about my money?*

The potential that my life savings could be at risk was too terrifying to consider, so I buried that final question and focused on getting the feeling back in my body. With an important meeting starting in an hour, it wasn't the time to have an emotional breakdown. I grabbed my bag, locked my car and got in a lift. When I stepped into the lobby, my phone dinged letting me know I'd missed a call from an unknown number. Then, another ping. The same caller had sent a text message.

Unknown: Tracy – please call me back urgently on this number. – Chris (Hamish's brother-in-law)

Instead of turning right to head to my office like usual, I went left, burst through the front doors and immediately called the number back. The morning sounds of buses, birds and business-as-usual all disappeared when Chris answered the phone. The only thing I could hear myself asking was one of the few questions that had *definitely* not been running through my mind that morning.

'Chris, who the fuck is Hamish?'

CHAPTER 1

The Fairytale

A lot of people rip on Disney for frequently killing one if not both parents in their movies, but I'm going to argue it's actually a good thing. For as confronting as it is to watch Bambi's mum bleed out in the snow or Simba's dad get double-crossed by his brother, it shows kids (and reminds hungover parents on a Sunday morning) that death, grief and hardship can happen to anyone, at any moment, and are unfortunately a part of life. While I'm sure Disney was hoping storylines with a side of trauma would guarantee a box-office blockbuster, I like to think they also wanted to help kids become empathetic, understand the importance of friendship and begin to develop resilience. Unfortunately for me, the writers weren't quite explicit enough when it came to *how* one should do that last part.

Thankfully, they say resilience is like a muscle – you build it over time. In my case, it took more time than I would have liked but without the challenges I faced in my late teens, I'm not sure I would have been able to handle what would eventually unfold in my twenties. And without the resilience that I had to continue to build throughout my thirties, I'm not sure I would have been able to stay upright when I finally figured out who the fuck Hamish was in my forties. But before I get into the juicy bits of how I became his famous 'last victim', I want to retrace the path I walked to show you that it doesn't matter where you were born, how you were raised or who you became as an adult – anyone can end up falling prey to a con.

If you're someone who grew up in the 70s and 80s, there's a good chance that you thought your happily ever after would look a lot like Cinderella and Prince Charming's or Jennifer Parker and Marty McFly's. I will also go out on a limb and say that a chunk of us were also hoping for a glow-up à la Sandy in *Grease* so we could snag a Danny Zuko. Even though I was born in 1975 and am proud to have these pop culture references ingrained in my DNA, my idea of happily ever after didn't look anything like glass slippers, self-lacing shoes or heels simply made to stomp out a cigarette. As corny as this sounds, the fairytale ending I wanted was playing out in front of my eyes in the form of my mum and dad.

Look, some people want a knight in shining armour … I wanted a nuclear family in a shining frame. Traditional in every sense of the word, the home I grew up in and the relationship I saw modelled to me were full of adoration, respect, humour and warmth. After falling in love and getting married, Mum, a physiotherapist, and Dad, a diesel mechanic, moved from Sydney up to northern New South

Wales and quickly got to work bringing two boys and me into the world. When I was five, we moved inland to Bilambil Heights where we stayed until I was eleven. Then Dad, who wanted to run his own business, decided to set up shop in Brisbane. We moved to the northern end of the Gold Coast, which is where I spent my formative years. Mum ran a tight ship at home, Dad worked long hours at his business and us kids were heavily scheduled with sport, academics, debating and musicals. Yet when we were having family lunch on Sundays, Mum and Dad's hands were always clasped, laughter was abundant and love was palpable. Often referred to as Snugglepot and Cuddlepie, they were truly the cutest little dumplings on this side of the Great Dividing Range.

As a kid, this dynamic felt safe. As a teen, it felt a tad vanilla but still nice. As a young adult, it felt sensible. But how many twenty-somethings typically lean into sensible? Let's be honest, when your prefrontal cortex isn't fully developed, you mostly go for the people who give you the biggest dopamine hit. So while my parents were spending their early empty-nester years going for long drives and sharing a bag of prawns by the beach, I was busy going on first dates, wiping tears from first heartbreaks and getting up to my fair share of mischief with friends and work colleagues. By the time I was twenty-seven, I'd experienced all sorts of love ... Right-Person-Wrong-Time Love, Gap-Year-in-London Love, More-Lust-Than-Love Love and, of course, Unrequited Love. All beautiful in their own ways, I knew that none of them were the Fairytale Love my parents set the bar for. Confident it would one day come,

I embraced being single and enjoyed the fact that I, at least, had Work Love.

To be clear, I wasn't hooking up with a co-worker. I'm talking about my love affair with marketing that started in 1998 when I was offered my dream job at Stadium Australia. I'd just graduated from Southern Cross University with a sports science degree and was tasked with helping Sydney host the 2000 Olympic Games. From the time I could toddle onto a field, playing and watching sport gave me life, which is why I spent most of 1999 and 2000 walking around Sydney Olympic Park soaking up every sight and sound it had to offer. Honestly, some days I worried my eyes were stuck open in awe because of what I was seeing, doing and learning. As a diehard Wallabies fan, the best part was being allowed on the sideline during the Bledisloe Cup … and trying to sneak into the changerooms without an access pass. This was when they were at the height of their rugby reign so you can best believe I wasn't going to blink and miss any of it.

When the opening ceremony commenced, I happened to be doing bridesmaid duty at a friend's wedding but was instantly filled with pride when I watched the replay. Not only did I have a deep admiration for the athletes walking in the Parade of Nations, but it was also fun knowing that I got to contribute to an event that the whole world would experience. The significance of Australia getting this honour was not lost on me. I took it all very seriously and worked like crazy.

But then the games ended and the suburb of Homebush lost its near-intoxicating Olympic buzz. Feeling the need for a new challenge, I gravitated to the finance world, taking a job with a start-up hedge fund. Full disclosure – I knew nothing about hedge funds and not a great deal more about finance in general. Money wasn't a big topic of discussion over the dinner table when I was growing up and Mum and Dad certainly never discussed their personal finances in front of us. While we never went without, I could tell that things weren't always easy and that my parents had to work very hard for what we had.

Seeing as I only had three years of experience, the company's CEO, Deon, graciously took a chance on mini marketing me. I admitted it then and I admit it now: I was totally winging it in the beginning. Due to how lean and green the start-up was, I quickly became Head of Marketing, which I found both hilarious and daunting. A true baptism by fire, I had to quickly learn the ins and outs of web design and investor relationships. Shortly after we became the first company to ever list a hedge fund on the stock exchange, I also had to learn the art of product disclosure documents and shareholder communication.

It could have been because I was working in the finance industry, or the fact that a few pay rises meant there was actual cash to spare, but saving and future-planning quickly became top of mind. For nearly thirty years, I'd watched my parents sacrifice their social lives, holidays and hobbies so that they could give my brothers and me a comfortable home, healthy food, too many sport shoes to count, as well as the gift of education. It was now my turn to be the responsible adult. But then something happened that made me ask: *What's the point?*

My dad got sick. At fifty-three, Dad was just about to reach the rainbow of retirement and had grand plans to spend it with Mum grey-nomading around Australia. One morning out of the blue, he started experiencing pain in his legs. Never one to make a fuss, he didn't mention it until an episode felt so severe that he went to the hospital the following day. Further testing showed that he had acute myeloid leukaemia (AML) and would need to begin treatment immediately.

The moment I heard he was unwell, I knew that I needed to get to the Gold Coast as soon as possible. Unfortunately, my brain was firing conflicting thoughts like a spray of shots from an assault rifle. *I'm overreacting. I'm underreacting. I'm not going to make it home in time. He's going to be completely fine. I can leave work. This is not the time to leave work.* Thankfully, Deon was there to order a ceasefire in my mind. Upon hearing my dad's diagnosis and prognosis, he put a company credit card in my hand to book a flight and assured me everything at work would be fine without me.

When I touched down on the Gold Coast, my friend and second mum, Lorraine, picked me up. I had met Lorraine when I was fourteen through a self-esteem seminar that she was running. Essentially a crash course in emotional intelligence for teens, I learned about limiting beliefs, reframing and the many ways you can increase your sense of self-worth. Perhaps the most important thing I learned was how helpful it can be to have a non-parental adult in your life who 'gets you'. Sure, I could talk to my parents about teen stuff but sometimes I needed to talk to someone about parent stuff. In the following years, Lorraine became my mentor, maker of fun and other mother when needed. At this moment, she was exactly who I needed to even begin to fathom the possibility of having to function in a world without my dad. Ever wise and generous with her spiritual beliefs, she gave me the courage I needed to step onto the footpath when she pulled up in front of the hospital.

For how desperate I'd been to get to my dad's side, I briefly hesitated at the entrance. Was I ready to see what was inside? With the aid of a few deep breaths, I willed my feet to move and found myself at yet another doorway. The lights inside Dad's hospital room were dimmed and it was very quiet. I concluded Mum must have stepped away for a moment as I watched my dad's belly rise and fall on the bed. As a young man, Dad was svelte and athletic. As an adult, Dad was smiley and, as Gran would say, 'had been in good pastures'. But even with his rotund physique still evident, there was a vulnerability and weakness about him I'd never seen. I took a step through the doorway. Dad looked up and smiled as I outstretched my arms and gave him a hug that I never wanted to end. When we finally prised ourselves apart, Dad stared deep into my soul and made a statement that had me wondering if he had a knowing that he was nearing his end.

'Look after Mum, okay?'

I looked into his eyes and searched for the always optimistic man I knew and loved. It didn't matter how I tilted my head or squinted my eyelids, I could only see fear. It felt very uncomfortable. In an attempt to rush past the feeling as quickly as possible, I promised to look after Mum and then did my best to convince Dad (and myself) that this really was just a blip on the radar.

'Before you know it, you and Mum will be waving from the Winnebago to take your triumphant retirement lap around Australia.'

Three weeks later, he died.

We were in disbelief. To be fair, denial is probably a more accurate word, but here's the thing: no-one told us that Dad was facing imminent death. Albeit gruelling, his chemotherapy was going according to plan and most of us just assumed that getting legal documents into place was precautionary or, at the worst, something we'd only need temporarily. Just days after Dad had shaved his head due to the rapid hair loss, I had even felt confident enough to briefly leave his side in order to attend the wedding of one of my closest friends. My work wife from my Stadium Australia days, Anita, was marrying her high school sweetheart, Baz, on the Sunshine Coast. Even though I wasn't in the mood for celebrating anything at that point, I was truly grateful to get to witness their union and feel their love and support.

When Dad's pain got bad enough to warrant high doses of morphine, it was clear that he had gone away with the fairies. Worried he wouldn't come back, we consulted the doctor, who reassured us that things often need to get worse before they get better and that we didn't need to be alarmed. Every day for the next week, we held our breaths and clung to hope that he'd miraculously wake up well and not sound like he was tripping on acid. But then one morning, Mum and I showed up and his room was empty. In a complete panic, we ran to the nurses' station and asked where Dad was. Apparently, things had taken a turn for the worse overnight. His organs were shutting down and he'd been transferred to the ICU just minutes before.

Instantly, I turned to every higher power I could think of and began silently praying. Aside from prayer, there was really nothing my family could do except sit in the agony of waiting for a miracle. For hours, we felt our butts, legs and hearts go numb. Just before 5 pm, a nurse led us to a family conference room. It quickly became obvious that news of miracles didn't occur there. A pair of doctors read Dad's health stats like a captain and co-pilot preparing for take-off.

'Are you saying that Andy might die tonight?' Mum asked.

The lack of eye contact and non-committal mumbling that sounded a lot like 'yes' confirmed that it was time to take turns saying our goodbyes and to notify extended family.

Up until this point, everything I knew about saying goodbye to a loved one in hospital had come from movies. While part of me just wanted to crawl into bed with Dad and sob, the other part of me wished I had more time to write an Oscar-worthy speech for him. I wanted to tell him how much I loved feeling his love. I wanted to tell him that I believed in true love and happily ever after because of the way he was with Mum. I wanted to tell him that just when I thought I couldn't admire him anymore, he'd do or say something that showed a depth to him that made me want to spend my lifetime trying to understand.

In the end, I didn't crawl into bed with him and I didn't say anything out loud. When I walked into his room, I listened to machines buzz and beep while my dad's shrunken belly barely rose with the assistance of a ventilator. I stood beside his bed, clasped his hand and thought about how much I was going to miss him. I also thought about how hard life is. I wouldn't say I'm a stoic but I've always been aware that adversity, trauma and grief don't discriminate. *Why wouldn't I lose a parent? Everyone loses their parents someday.* Still, it all felt wildly unfair.

Once the rest of my family members had had their goodbyes with Dad, Mum and I drove home in silence and crawled into my bed together. Periodically, we'd feel each other's bodies shaking as tears began to fall. My heart was broken in ways I could never have imagined. Yes, I was devastated by the loss of my dad, but the pain I felt for Mum was equally intense. I imagined her having to face the bedroom they'd shared for over thirty years, the mail that would keep coming for Mr Andrew Hall, as well as the procession of people who'd no doubt show up to the funeral offering words they knew wouldn't take away a fraction of her pain.

At 5 am, the phone rang. Mum answered, listened, thanked whoever was on the other end and then hung up.

'He's gone,' she whispered.

Stunned and silent, the crying consumed us.

CHAPTER 2

The Nightmare

When I was sixteen, I found myself floating above my body in the middle of the night. I was conscious that something was pulling me away from my bedroom, yet I was surprisingly calm when I reached the stars. For how far I felt from Earth, I could still clearly see the outline of my curled legs under my blanket and a pile of not-ready-for-the-wash-but-not-ready-to-be-put-away-again clothes on the floor. Just when I started to worry that I might be drifting too far away, I noticed a cord that was evidently keeping me tethered to my body. Seconds later, my eyes cracked open and I was back in my room. Thinking it was simply a weird dream, I told Dad about it over breakfast the next morning.

'That sounds a bit like astral travelling.'

Mid-bite of Weet-Bix, my mouth instantly became agape. 'Astral travelling?'

As if this was just an everyday conversation, Dad explained what astral travelling was, adding that he had a book about it if I wanted to learn more. Seeing as Dad was a child of the 60s and 70s, I shouldn't have been shocked and yet, this was one of those rare occasions where he managed to make me feel like I was only scratching the surface of who he really was. Could it be that he was a diesel mechanic by day and amateur occult cosmologist by night?

Dad's bookshelf offered the greatest insight into his psyche. As a toddler, I could really only explore the bottom two shelves, which held the obligatory *Encyclopaedia Britannica* set that we all relied on before Google. As I got taller, I learned that there are two types of parents in the world: parents who have 'the talk' and parents who leave books such as *Where Did I Come From?* and *What's Happening to Me?* at a ten-year-old's eye level. (And the ones who have a copy of *The Joy of Sex* in their bedside table drawer.) By the time I was in high school and had confirmed my suspicions that I was not left on my parents' doorstep by a stork, my fingers graduated to the pages of Dad's top-shelf books such as *The Happy Hooker, The Richest Man in Babylon* and *Jonathan Livingston Seagull.* I was so enthralled by the stories of madams, merchants and soaring to great heights that it's understandable I hadn't noticed the unassuming copy of *The Art and Practice of Astral Projection* which Dad handed to me before heading to work.

Over the next few years, I read parts of it here and there. I learned that multiple cultures, religions and mythologies share similar beliefs that the soul or consciousness can hover over the physical body and, in some cases, travel throughout the astral realm. Also called 'astral projection', it's thought that this out-of-body state can be reached through meditation, hypnosis, ancient rituals and, of course, some hallucinogens. Even though it was fun to imagine my soul being able to have astral experiences, I didn't feel compelled to try to intentionally leave my body. But when my dad died, I suddenly wanted nothing more than to master astral travelling so that I could find any possible way to connect with him one last time. Unfortunately, 'Find Your Dad's Soul in the Astral Realm and Say the Things That Were Left Unsaid' was not on my list of things to do in the days following his passing.

Instead, I had to pull myself up from crying on the floor and make the many 'Dad's passed' phone calls I'd been dreading. After that, I gathered photos and footage for a memorial slideshow (while trying not to care that all these jobs seemed to be falling on me.) Most importantly, I needed to stand by Mum as she made plans to bury the love of her life. Growing up, I thought funerals were held to pay tribute to the life of a newly departed while simultaneously helping the bereaved accept the reality that their loved one was truly gone. I still think this is the case but planning my dad's funeral made me suspect that its most important purpose is to get immediate family members busy. When you're busy, you're less likely to succumb to the wounds of a broken heart or dwell on the question we silently ask after someone we love dies: *What's the point of going on?*

For as mundane as planning a wake menu and writing dates on frozen meals can feel, it's actually a key way to survive. When your conscious mind is distracted by the busyness of deciding 'this chaplain, that coffin and lilies not carnations', your subconscious mind gets the time needed to triage internal damage, compartmentalise traumatic memories and overwhelming emotions, and ultimately do what needs to be done so that you are able to stay upright when grief inevitably takes hold. Look, a wake menu may just be a wake menu, but when my body was trying to make sense of my world without my dad, it was a lifeline.

Due to the fact that the only thing my family worshipped was sport, Dad's funeral was held at a non-denominational memorial centre in Carrara on the Gold Coast. For how significant this day was, I actually can't remember the details that clearly. Each scene plays out like it was filmed through a lens coated in grease; however, I do recall the immense support and love I felt when family, friends and colleagues showed up from across Australia. I also recall the wave of sadness that hit everyone when Dad's mother, Gran, was ushered in to farewell her youngest son.

The thing that I definitely recall was the energy shift that happened to my family when we could no longer find ways to be busy. My family, who weren't and aren't particularly touchy-feely, used this shift to keep calm, carry on and avoid acknowledging the grief we were feeling. After Dad's body was cremated and the formalities of the funeral were finalised, Mum, my brothers and I shared fun and happy 'Dad memories', but anything that reminded us of our pain was often swept under the rug.

Every atom in my body ached when I thought about my future husband and kids not getting to meet the man who had hung the moon and stars in my universe, so I was more than happy to play the game of grief avoidance.

But here's the thing about grief: it can and will show up in your dreams, your lungs, your gut, your heart and even your knees if you don't eventually acknowledge it. Essentially a Kardashian of emotions, grief comes in many different shapes and sizes, wants all the attention and is not going to take no for an answer.

Of course, I didn't know any of this at twenty-six. I just wanted to go 'back to normal' but there was nothing normal about how I was feeling and what I was thinking during that time. In all honesty, I figured that grief was just sadness on steroids; nothing two days off work couldn't fix. Well, let me tell you, two days off work came and went and to my horror, I wasn't just still sad, I was convinced I was experiencing early onset dementia. On multiple occasions, I forgot to get off the ferry while commuting from work and even when I was on the clock, I could barely remember how to do my job. I made loads of mistakes and was emotionally unhinged. I chalked up most of my physical ailments, including brain fog, forgetfulness and extreme fatigue, to exhaustion. Sleep became an elusive lover while the quietness of my room at 2 am was a newfound friend.

It could have been my upbringing or Australia's social landscape at the time, but I thought grieving was something that had to be done in private. I didn't get grief counselling, I didn't take any time off work and I didn't do a hell of a lot of self-care. I just tried to get on with it. For as far as we've come as a society that's historically not taught its members how to grieve, we're still incredibly uncomfortable with it. At home, I felt free to stare vacantly at a wall, lie in the foetal position on my shower floor or audibly bargain with the universe. But when with friends or out in public, I was always either 'Doing okay!' or 'Getting there!' My journal entries devolved from my usual outpourings of gratitude and hope for the future into lines like, *I feel very lonely right now. I don't want to be alone but I don't want to be surrounded by people either. I am so tired and sad. I wish there was something I could do, something I could say to everyone to make it all better, but all I come up with is nothing. Nothing useful anyway. Only more questions and sadness. Just an alone feeling ... a nothing feeling. Sometimes, I wish I was with Dad.*

Some of my darkest days came on the first 'withouts'. In September, I had my first Father's Day without Dad. In November, I had my first birthday without Dad. And in December, my mum, brothers and I had our first Christmas without Dad. We tried to make it fun and happy, but the underpinning sadness was screaming at us to just stop pretending that everything was okay. During those first few trips back home, I fully expected Dad to walk through the door in his Akubra and kiss me hello. Even when I was in Sydney, I'd find myself reaching for my phone to text Dad about something funny before remembering that he was *really* gone.

The hardest first 'without' came on New Year's Eve – Dad's birthday. Anita and Baz, who were still in newlywed bliss, invited me to a party at their new river house in Brisbane. As wonderful as the distraction of a bonfire by the river with friends and fermented beverages sounded, I didn't want Mum to be on her own. As the final day of 2002 drew to a close, Mum and I ate birthday cake for

Dad, raised a glass of champagne and watched the Sydney Harbour Bridge fireworks light up the TV. Through tears, we toasted the arrival of 2003 while silently trying to accept the departure of life as we once knew it.

Exactly one week later, I was on my way to work on the ferry. With a strong soy latte in hand, I took a seat in my favourite spot outside to feel the sun on my face and sea spray from the chop. When I remembered to get off at my stop, I felt a sense of pride and thought, *Look at me go! Perhaps I'm coming out of my grief coma!* I arrived at my desk at 8 am after the short walk from Circular Quay to Bligh Street. Just when I was feeling like the smile on my face might be genuine, my phone rang. Before I could finish saying hello, Anita screamed through the phone, 'Baz is dead!' He'd had a seizure and died in his sleep next to her.

The scaffolding that I'd so carefully constructed around myself, along with the veils of my 'okay-ness', came crashing down on the cold tiles of the company toilets. I couldn't feel my legs, I felt like vomiting, my arms were shaking and then everything went dark. When I could see again, I felt the arms of a colleague helping me sit up. I think the technical term for this is 'shock', but 'post-traumatic grief bomb' feels more accurate. When I heard the unthinkable words from Anita that Baz was dead, every emotion I had experienced (as well as the emotions that I had refused to experience) over the last six months came rushing through my veins. Eventually I was able to stand and make my way back to my desk to try to process the un-processable.

Once again, I found my boss Deon by my side handing me a credit card and telling me to go home and be with my friends and family. I went straight into grief-shock-busy mode and put myself on the first available plane to Brisbane.

When I wasn't using all of my energy to appear strong for Anita's sake, I couldn't help but notice that without the busyness of funeral planning, there were two questions getting louder and louder in my head.

What's the point of working twelve-hour days for thirty years when there's every chance I could follow in my dad's footsteps and be taken out by leukaemia at fifty-three?

What's the point of falling in love with someone when there's every chance that they will be ripped from my life while sleeping next to me in bed at thirty-one?

In the months following Baz's funeral, I attempted to answer these questions when I couldn't keep busy enough to avoid them. My mind spiralled on my lunch breaks as I spent the entire hour walking through the streets near my office with tears streaming down my face, in what can best be described as a grief-fuelled haze. In hindsight, food, a nap or social contact would probably have been the better choice. Even on the days I thought I could hold myself together, I always seemed to find a reason to cry. I'd see an elderly couple sitting on a bench or a young family picnicking in a park and my mind would immediately flash to Dad and Baz. I'd think about how hard they worked for love and financial security only for it all to be lost almost instantly. Seconds later, any viable answers I had managed to come up with were decimated.

The more I had to fight back tears on these walks, the more I wondered why 'Grief Rooms' weren't a thing.

Where are people supposed to go when they can't hold back their tears in public? My grieving became harder to keep private, but thankfully, I could always rely on 2 am and my bedroom ceiling to shield the world from witnessing the true depths of my sorrow. *What is the point?* became my mantra. To be clear, I wasn't suicidal or even feeling hopeless. I fully believed that my life was worth living. I had a great job, strong family, incredible friends, good health and confidence that I would meet someone who'd be the Snugglepot to my Cuddlepie. I was just frozen with fear and sadness because I couldn't see how I was going to get through the debilitating pain that comes with loss and also become comfortable with knowing that it's inevitable. Really, I had lost my drive.

CHAPTER 3

My Future According to Grains of Rice

It was 7.38 pm on a Tuesday evening when the cynic inside me took over my brain. *I knew it. You're dying and you're not even thirty. You've just spent a decade of your life working non-stop so you can one day buy a house for the family you'll never have …*

In my cynic's defence, anyone watching me do my evening shop at the supermarket after work would have assumed I was dying. I was standing in the dairy aisle contemplating the price of organic butter when I suddenly became boiling hot. Today, I can compare it to menopausal night sweats that make you rip off your duvet, pyjamas and will to live, but at the time, it felt like someone was taking every single nerve ending in my body and holding it over fire. Before I could even acknowledge the ringing in my ears, I lost feeling in my arms. My legs felt like jelly, my heart was beating out of my chest and my shopping basket hit the floor. I attempted to bend down and pick up the glaringly obvious dinner-for-one ingredients, but the heat radiating through my body was too much. I had to get outside.

Spoiler alert: I didn't die. This was just the first of multiple panic attacks I'd have before deciding to quit my job and go travelling through India and Nepal with Anita. It has been said that there are two places you need to go often: the place that heals you and the place that inspires you. Of course, I didn't know this was what I was doing when I slipped my feet into a well-worn pair of Birkenstocks, grabbed my free-with-(rarely used)-gym-membership backpack and made sure my passport was zipped securely in an internal pocket. Look, I could *Eat, Pray, Love* you and say that we were going to India and Nepal in pursuit of a spiritual awakening but the truth is I simply wanted to escape the grip that grief had on me. I was hoping for a geographical cure or, at the very least, a distraction. The plan: I would volunteer at an orphanage in Kathmandu, Nepal, trek the famous Annapurna Circuit and teach English at a slum school in a village outside of Bangalore, India.

By the time I arrived in Nepal in mid-2003, Anita had already begun volunteering at the orphanage. Because I wanted to do the Annapurna Circuit trek while the weather was still warm, I delayed my volunteering and put myself on a bus to Pokhara with a Flemish-speaking, Belgium-dwelling German backpacker I nicknamed the 'Jolly German'. Having only just met this curly-headed good time at a bar in Kathmandu and learning that he, too, had dreams of exploring central Nepal's mountain ranges, he seemed like the perfect stranger to embark on a three-week trek with. Since good things come in threes, we convinced the only other foreigner on our bus to join us – a very dreamy yet very smelly guy I secretly called the 'French Dream' (it didn't matter that he smelled like a buffalo's arse, he was hot with a sexy accent).

Once in Pokhara, the Jolly German, French Dream and I found a willing and seemingly knowledgeable man, Chandra, to be our guide. With backpacks fully loaded and our hiking boots laced up tight, we walked day after day high up into the Himalayas. Some days we spoke of only fodder or foot pain. Other times, we discussed the Maoist government and political climate or recounted stories from back home and learned about each other's lives. It was there on those tracks that I finally felt like I was in a place where I could be me without any attachments. I wasn't the girl who worked in finance who'd just lost her dad and friend. I was the girl who could lap up the energy of two strangers and the magic that is Mother Earth.

As we walked through villages and wild marijuana fields, I felt an incredible high. (From the experience, not the abundant crops brushing against my knees.) Just one kilometre from Thorong La, which is 5416 metres above sea level and one of the only peaks you can do without oxygen containers, my high became one I desperately needed to come down from. I had altitude sickness and it was becoming increasingly bad. To put it into context, Thorong La is higher than Everest Base Camp, which sits at 5364 metres. Even though I was fit, strong and healthy,

I don't think I had prepared my body well enough to handle the altitude. In fact, I know I didn't because as Chandra, the Jolly German and French Dream happily plodded up that last ascent, I was pausing to have conversations with all the people I was seeing in what I soon learned were wild hallucinations. The higher we got, the sicker I got. When the nausea set in, my nose started bleeding and my head felt like it was going to explode, I knew it was time to call it quits. Every part of me wanted to push on, but I also wanted to live. We all agreed it was better for me to walk down than to be carried down in a body bag, so it was decided that Chandra would accompany me back to Manang. I would rest and recover before making my way to Pokhara to meet back up with the Jolly German and French Dream.

Altitude sickness aside, my first few weeks in Nepal were great and set the tone for what the rest of the year would bring. It didn't matter if I was in the slums of India or having lunch with backpackers in a city square, I was pushed out of my comfort zone, given the chance to connect with people I may never have had the opportunity to cross paths with and, ultimately, discovered that I hadn't lost my drive when my dad and Baz died; I'd simply gained some much-needed perspective. Perspective that was quickly compounded by the many kids I came in contact with.

In India, Anita and I volunteered at a slum school where food, uniforms, medical care, books and school supplies were provided. We taught kids who'd been maimed by their own parents to make them more effective beggars. We taught kids who slept huddled together in alleyways at night. Some of these kids were avoiding the wrath of an alcoholic parent while others didn't even have a parent to avoid. Regardless of their circumstance, these kids still showed up to school smiling and eager to learn.

The experiences I had in Nepal and India could be a book on their own, so I will summarise the part where Anita and I ventured to Amritapuri, an ashram full of navel-gazing Westerners who'd taken vows of silence, forgone food and devoted themselves to a spiritual guru known as Amma, The Mother of All. (And had also paid huge sums of money to wear matching white outfits.) Long story short – we were terrible disciples who lasted less than twenty-four hours. I will also gloss over our quick visit to McLeod Ganj near Dharamshala during Diwali – except for the part where tealight candles illuminated each step of the mud stairs we took from our hostel to hear the man, the myth, the legend himself – THE Dalai Lama – speak. It was epic. But the one story I cannot bypass is the one that involved a witch doctor, a bag of rice and a fortune that wouldn't make sense until writing this very book.

In a cafe in Durbar Square, Patan, Anita and I celebrated the birthday of our friend, Rina, who ran the orphanage where we were working in Nepal. Anita and I asked Rina whether she could take us to see a clairvoyant or tarot reader. Just as Rina had an answer for every question we asked at the orphanage, be it about daily logistics or the complicated world of NGOs in Nepal, she knew exactly who we needed to go to: the local healer. Before I knew it, we were huddled in a tiny room in a little house alongside what felt like half the village and a man who was more witch doctor than healer in my eyes.

After doing a mental inventory of the myriad snake skins hanging from the ceiling and walls and incense sticks dropping ashes on every surface, I waited in the corner cradling a small bag of rice, which was evidently the witch doctor's preferred payment method. Numerous women and children took turns kneeling on a single straw mat in front of him in an effort to put on weight, become pregnant, end bad luck or heal their broken hearts. Dressed in a white button-down shirt, grey striped linen pants and what I'm almost positive was the same silver digital Seiko watch my high school maths teacher used to wear, the witch doctor's voice would increase several decibels as he poured each person's rice grains onto a tray for his fingers to run through and begin his reading.

Chanting information that clearly indicated doctor–patient confidentiality was not a thing in the Nepalese witch doctor world, he'd whack their heads with a straw broom, have them drink tonics that looked like they'd been concocted from tar, pond water and bin juice and, depending on how dark their future looked, tell them to wear a necklace that held tiger whiskers inside a hollow silver bullet for thirty months or until it fell off naturally. Rina, who'd been translating at rapid speed, explained this would help ward off the evil spirits heading their way.

When it was finally time for me (and the rest of the room) to hear my fate, I silently prayed that the witch doctor wouldn't make me swallow anything more than the information that was going to come out of his mouth. Just two people before me, he'd mixed a potion of oils and herbs with his fingers right there on the floor ... Thankfully, my mind couldn't focus on the possible bacteria looming in my future because the witch doctor's straw broom began repeatedly whacking my head and face as he spoke.

Rina translated:

You're twenty-seven.

Scorpio.

You have no father.

Two brothers.

You will be respected for your work and not money.

You enjoy working with and for poor people.

You will have four children: two boys and two girls.

For the next thirty months, you'll have bad luck and should be careful of accidents.

You will give your money carelessly and therefore will have financial problems.

At the time, I was blown away that the witch doctor knew my age, star sign and family details. But like most women who read their daily horoscope, I morphed his just-vague-enough positive fortunes to directly apply to my life at that moment. As for the negative ones ... like the one about me giving money carelessly and having financial problems? I simply tucked it away in my journal and didn't think about it again. However, when he placed a necklace around my neck to help ward off evil spirits, I decided it wouldn't hurt to keep it on until it fell off naturally.

When I returned to Australia at the end of 2003, I showed up on my mum's doorstep with a new nose ring, new perspective and new plan. Instead of moving back to Sydney and resuming my place in the rat race, I'd stay with her on the Gold Coast and find a local marketing job. (One with a company that was cool with nose rings and tiger whisker necklaces, obviously.) After witnessing the disparities between my life in urban Australia and a life in the slums, I understood how lucky I was to have the opportunity to not just earn money, but to also have the privilege of being able to stay close to my family. Perhaps the most important thing I came home with was a renewed sense of hope. I was determined to focus on what I did have, not what I didn't. While I knew that my once all-consuming grief would never fully be gone, I was grateful to notice that it was lying dormant for longer and longer stretches of time. In fact, it stayed dormant long enough for me to fall in love.

CHAPTER 4

Marriage and Motherhood

By the time thirty months had passed since the witch doctor laid out my future in grains of rice, I felt like I couldn't be further away from bad luck. If anything, I felt like the most fortunate woman in the world because I was sure that I had finally found my happily ever after. Shortly after returning from India, I met my very own Prince Charming. Tall, dark, handsome and someone a romance novelist might describe as 'mesmerising', this prince swept me off my feet when I was in Sydney for a girlfriend's hen's weekend. After six months of long distance, the gravitational pull of our connection convinced me it was time to move back and accept the pace that our relationship was taking.

'Fast fun' is the best way to describe what we had. It didn't matter where we were, who we were with or what we were doing; it was always a really good time. Our thirties brought us trips overseas, more hangovers than I care to remember and countless weekends spent with big groups of friends. They also brought us a beautiful wedding in the Byron Bay hinterland, a four-week honeymoon in Thailand and Singapore, an 80s beach shack that would one day become our 'forever home' in Freshwater, Sydney, and two pink lines on a pregnancy test. For all the joy that we'd experienced together, nothing compared to the elation we felt when we became parents to our daughter, Asha, in 2010. In Hindi, Asha means 'hope'. And that's exactly what she would give me just weeks after she was born.

People told me that motherhood would temporarily turn me into a sleep-deprived milk machine with little concern for my personal hygiene and they weren't wrong. Thankfully, Mum was there to help me survive those early newborn days that don't seem to have a beginning, middle or end. When she wasn't rocking Asha to sleep or starting yet another load of washing, she was typically holding me while I sobbed as my nipples bled and my caesarean scar ached. Sometimes I was crying because my love for Asha was overwhelming. Other times it was because I'd watched a Qantas commercial. After three weeks of giving my little family the most incredible care, Mum needed to go home. Always one to keep herself busy, Mum's golf plans, Scrabble club meet-ups and volunteering duties were calling.

Two weeks after Mum left, Asha hit the five-week mark and I found myself standing in our kitchen afraid to make a single move. It was 6.09 am and Asha had just achieved her longest stretch of sleep yet. I remember thinking, 'Dare I risk waking her in pursuit of a cup of tea that I get to drink while it's still hot or do I just bask in the glory of a sleeping baby?' I chose glory, which lasted all of seven minutes but was absolutely worth it. Later that day, I was taking advantage of yet another unusually long stretch of sleep when Mum called. Fully expecting her to tell me about her day on the golf course or ask me what Asha's latest milestone was, I couldn't have been more confused when I heard the words, 'They've found some cells.'

'What cells? What do you mean? Do you mean cancer?' I asked in rapid succession. The phone went silent and all I could think was, *Fuck, here we go again. Please God, no. I can't.*

I was confused by this information for a number of reasons. For starters, if you looked up 'strong constitution' in the encyclopaedia set that Mum only recently threw away, I'm confident you'd find a picture of her as a reference. This woman *never* got sick. I don't know if it was because of her healthy lifestyle choices or simply the fact that she didn't have time because she had three kids, but my brothers and I cannot recall her even having a runny nose. In fact, the only time we suspected a weakness was when we were due to go to the zoo as a family but had to cancel because Mum hurt her back and needed to lie in a hot bath all day. Mum being noticeably unwell literally happened once in my whole childhood.

To say I was broken by the news that Mum had been diagnosed with breast cancer is an understatement. *I can't lose you too. Not now.*

When we hung up, I heard a now-very-awake Asha and went to pick her up. As soon as she was in my arms, my tears were streaming down onto her little head. Suddenly,

I felt my heart and head flood with hope. *You're the point, just keep going.*

Just like with Dad, I was on a plane and in hospital by Mum's side the day following her mastectomy. It could have been the exorbitant levels of oestrogen coursing through my veins but the stark reality that I might lose my mum just as I'd become a mum was infinitely more difficult to accept. Luckily, Mum never made me feel like I had to accept that she might die. From the get-go, she remained calm, confident and (at least in front of me) complaint-free.

Instead of spending my maternity leave meeting other mums in the park, drinking coffee and comparing the sleep and shit patterns of our newborns, I spent mine flying solo with Asha up to Queensland as much as possible while Mum received chemo, radiation and, eventually, a hysterectomy. While I won't say that Mum breezed through treatment, she appeared as strong as an ox and never gave in to the thought that the Big C would get the better of her. Even when she shaved her head and chose to start wearing wigs, she seemed to take it all in stride. Now that I'm a mother myself, I suspect she protected and shielded us so fiercely because she didn't want her kids to suffer any more than we already had with the loss of Dad.

After nearly five years of treatment, Mum was deemed cancer-free. After seven, she was given the coveted 'remission' report. Before we knew it, she was back to being the mother and grandmother that Asha and I so desperately needed. On the days we need love, she knows what to say. On the days we need help, she knows what to do. On the days we need to be heard, she knows how to listen. And on the days when I need someone to help me mother Asha, she knows how to be the perfect amount of terrifying. Aptly nicknamed 'Nanny Bootcamp' (which somehow became 'Booty' over the years), this woman runs the tightest ship, takes no nonsense and firmly believes that there's no behavioural problem you can't (figuratively) knock out of a kid in three days. Bad sleeper? Fussy eater? Poo protester? Nanny Bootcamp is the answer. There's literally nothing she can't sort out.

Mum's love may sometimes be tough but it was also unconditional, infinite and exactly what I needed when Prince Charming and I learned that our second baby no longer had a heartbeat at our thirteen-week scan. The year was 2014 and Asha was nearly four. I was in tears when I rang Mum to tell her that we'd lost our baby. I could tell in the shakiness of her voice that Mum was crying too. We both knew how much I'd wanted to have another baby. She comforted and consoled me and filled the spaces where I felt empty and lonely.

A few months after our miscarriage, I was back on the phone with Mum to say something I desperately didn't want to admit. The threads that had once held my marriage together were rapidly unravelling. For many years, I did everything I could to identify, understand, pinpoint, unpack and try to mend the many causes of why Prince Charming and I just couldn't 'be'. While I won't veer you off course (you're here for the part where I fall in love with the con man!), I will say this – I was drawn to Prince Charming because of the way he embraced life and could connect so easily with others. I loved the way he could light up a room and his energy was contagious. Initially, I found comfort and safety standing in his shadow. My fairytale simply ended because I inevitably realised that there are few things that can survive without light.

CHAPTER 5

Tracy, 40

If you think writing a book sounds daunting, you should try penning a dating app bio as a divorced mum of a six-year-old who hasn't been 'on the scene' since 2003.

Tracy, 40

As someone who's always on time for daycare drop-offs and never misses a deadline, I take great pride in my ability to juggle my career with the domestic drudgery that comes with being a single working parent. In my spare time, my hobbies include shuttling my daughter to gymnastics, netball, playdates and parties, as well as perfecting the art of making fairy cupcakes at midnight for a school event I've invariably forgotten about. If you're into messy mum buns and dissecting the psychology of Peppa Pig's family in your spare time, then I might just be your type. Please don't send me any photos you wouldn't send your mother, my kid gets my phone at cafes. Also important to know: I occasionally snort when I laugh and I'm the kind of person who kicks the rogue grape under the fridge knowing it will be a sultana snack when we move house in a few years. Don't judge me.

Okay, so I came up with something better than that for my Happn dating app profile and believe it or not, the eligible bachelors came rolling in. However, the RSI in my thumb will tell you that it was slim pickings. As I swiped left, left, left and left, it became evident that Von Dutch hats were out and pictures of men posing with sedated tigers in Thailand were in. It's safe to say 2016 was a confronting year for a lot of people. Donald Trump became the 45th President of the United States, the United Kingdom made its Brexit and I discovered in equal measures the exhilaration and the disappointment of the over-forties online dating world.

For my married friends, my newfound singlehood was met with excitement and envy. *Show me who you've matched with! Have you broken the seal yet? What's it like to stay up past 10 pm?* To be completely honest, I started out wide-eyed and optimistic too. It had taken me a long time to gain the courage to leave my marriage. Once I had, I knew I was finally clear on who I was and what I wanted in my life. I had done a lot of work to move beyond the grief of losing the marriage and family life I thought I was going to have. And so, I took a swan dive into the Sydney dating pool with the confidence of a seasoned swimmer, or at the very least, a kid with floaties.

In a city whose population pushed five million, I really thought that my phone would be filled with plenty of fish to choose from. Unfortunately, those clever demographic and location algorithms quickly turned my pool into a puddle and, more often than not, the most promising profile turned out to be someone who even Rex Hunt wouldn't kiss before throwing back into the ocean.

Here's the thing about dating in your forties as a single mum who works full-time – you have little time for actual dates, even less time for dickheads, and have to miraculously create time to take care of a few stray nipple hairs before taking things to second base. However, you still have the very human desire to love and be loved and are aware that some awesome guy isn't going to fall out of your ceiling while you're sitting on the lounge watching *Farmer Wants a Wife* on a Tuesday night (hairy nips and all). And so, you engage in the monotonous act of swiping your way through photos and descriptions of men who should be good in theory, but you'd never look twice at if you crossed paths on the street.

Jason, 43, made my thumb hover a little longer than usual. He had a great smile, age-appropriate clothing and was not posing in front of a sad animal. But then I saw it. 'It' being the matching floral Laura Ashley bedspread, bed skirts and lampshade. *Did he still live with his mum? Or worse, was his mum the one taking the picture?* Sigh. Left.

Aaron, 45, looked promising. He worked in banking and said he was an avid hiker. Upon meeting, I learned that Aaron had either forgotten to wear sunscreen his entire life or was, in fact, closer to sixty-five. Turns out it was the latter.

Mark, 43, was handsome and witty. The only issue was that he was married 'but looking for other opportunities'.

Sadly, his wife was unaware that they were in an open relationship. Even though my thumbs were exhausted, I did take the time to go to town on his behaviour and explained that he was the moral opposite of what I wanted in my life. Block.

Brad, 38, was adorable but turned out to be a gung-ho Ayurvedic massage therapist who masqueraded as a single guy as a way to solicit business. Even though I was actually impressed by his creativity and entrepreneurial flare, I wasn't sure mixing business with pleasure was going to end well for either of us.

Karl, 40, was the first one to blindside me with a full frontal of his penis. (Yes, my first dick pic.) 'This is me right now.' As I looked at him standing in front of a full-length mirror proudly showing off his erection, I immediately thought, *What a load of bullshit. You're probably sitting on a toilet taking a dump and mass texting this poorly lit pic and unkempt bush to a bunch of random women across Australia. It's not even midday, Karl. I don't want to see a close-up of a dick and balls at the best of times, and definitely not right now and definitely not from you …* Block.

Jason, 40, wanted a picture of my body on a Monday night. Apparently, the close-up of my big toe did not suffice.

Kyle, 37, wanted to know twenty minutes after our first text what my address was so he could come over to have sex with me. That was also a Monday night. Monday Madness was a thing, it seemed. Sigh.

While my friends and I got really good laughs out of these stories, they'd go home to their husbands and I'd be left blocking the repeat dick pic offenders and casting more nets. Eventually, the whole endeavour started to feel soul-destroying because I was becoming increasingly aware of how much we judge other humans for being single. It was shocking how often I'd find myself thinking, *Why aren't they married? Why aren't they in a relationship? There must be something wrong with them.* And then I'd apply the same logic to myself and really spiral … *Why couldn't I make marriage work? Why am I not in a relationship? There must be something wrong with me.*

When the interactions were positive, it boosted my confidence and gave me a little dopamine hit. But mostly, it was demoralising, distracting and a monumental waste of time. Eventually, I let go of any expectations and simply hoped that I could at least meet some interesting people outside of my usual circles, go for a glass of wine and have some fun. Just when I was about to give up on the whole thing, I managed to make a few new friends.

There was Michael, 41, an ex-corporate executive who took a very delicious redundancy payout and was leaving in three months to open a boutique hotel in Puglia, Italy. Dave, 40, was an accountant who was keen to see plays, sport and try new restaurants. And Max, 41, was a blonder than blond Bondi surfer, triathlete and financial advisor who used correct grammar and found it entertaining that I'd taken three weeks to respond to his first message. While things with Michael and Dave fizzled, Max seemed to keep giving me a reason to check my phone. On average, it took about an hour on the express bus to get from my apartment in Freshwater to eBay's Sydney office, which thanks to

Max's knack for 'this or that' question-asking, I mostly spent deep in thought about my answers.

'*Top Gun* or *Dirty Dancing*?', 'Snow or sun?', 'Italian food or Japanese?'

I had instinctively typed, '*Dirty Dancing*, sun and Japanese' but paused before sending. I had to admit that there's something about the homoerotic beach volleyball scene in *Top Gun* that was putting Baby in the corner. And while I innately seek sunshine wherever I go, my mind flashed to the snow-capped Annapurna mountains that had soothed my soul in a way I never imagined was possible. As for Japanese, the sashimi and sake at Toko hold a special place in my heart … but gnocchi. The texture always feels right in your mouth. Ultimately, I went with my initial answers but appreciated the prompt to go within.

Our chats eventually deepened. I learned that Max had recently returned to Australia after doing a small stint in London and working in New York City for sixteen years. Unlike the stereotypical finance guys I had crossed paths with when working for that start-up hedge fund early in my career (e.g. the ones who seek status and pine for Patek Philippe watches), Max seemed to be seeking a quiet life and was only pining for endless surf breaks. He came across as humble and grateful for the chance to live in Bondi and work as the chief investment officer for a family office that looked after the multi-generational wealth of multiple families.

After a few weeks of proving that we were both able to commit to witty banter and swift (but not too eager) response times, Max asked if we could commit to a phone call. The first was planned to take place while I was in a cab to see the comedian Kitty Flanagan perform at the Enmore Theatre with my long-time friend Cath. I had met Cath in 2004 when she interviewed me for a role with the telecommunications company AAPT. Against the advice of the recruiter, I'd kept in the nose piercing I'd recently had done in India, which instantly caught Cath's eye and prompted her to ask all about my time volunteering. After I got the job, Cath told me it was my nose ring and gap in my CV that made me the winning applicant. From that moment on, we've been best friends.

Within minutes of being in the cab, my phone began vibrating on my lap. When I looked down and saw the name *Max Tavita* light up my phone, I felt the same butterflies in my stomach that I had when Mark Duckworth asked me out in Year 5. My mouth cracked into a smile before I answered. It's funny how foreign your own voice can sound when you're nervous. Thankfully, the cortisol coursing through my veins quickly dissipated. Max had a familiar Australian drawl and blokeyness to him that felt comfortable and fun. As the taxi crossed the Spit Bridge and wove its way through Neutral Bay, I answered questions about my work, family and hobbies. I shared the highlights of my marketing career, the lowlights of losing my father to leukaemia, the basics of my recent separation and that I had a six-year-old daughter living with me apart from Wednesdays and every other weekend. I spoke of my love of running, desire to travel and a virtual reality work project that was capturing most of my interest (and spare time) at the moment.

Somewhere near the Harbour Bridge, I asked Max about his family.

'My parents died in a plane crash when I was six.'

My mouth was instantly agape. 'I'm sorry to hear that,' I said.

'Don't worry. It was a long time ago.'

Max managed to sound upbeat and completely fine talking about such an unimaginable loss, but I could feel a heaviness hang on the line when he spoke about being separated from his two older sisters in the foster system. Since I was evidently struggling to find words, Max took over and shared that he'd ended up with a family in the Northern Beaches who had three boys and he'd had a very happy childhood. It's interesting how it's often the bereaved who have to comfort and reassure others.

Before I knew it, I was on the footpath in front of the Enmore Theatre holding my phone, wallet and a few unfamiliar feelings. Max had a down-to-earth energy about him, a great sense of humour and the ability to ask truly thoughtful questions without the urge to pontificate. It was a combination I'd never experienced from a prospective partner. I checked my phone and saw that we'd been chatting for more than forty-five minutes. I knew we needed to hang up, but the words were flowing so easily. After a prolonged goodbye, I slipped my phone into my bag and greeted Cath whose facial expression clearly said, 'Tell me everything!'

Giddy with excitement, I gave Cath the rundown over dinner after the show. When I got home a few hours later, I googled 'Tavita plane crash'. Weirdly, my search came up with nothing.

PART II

DURING

'What helps humanity survive doesn't always help the human, and our propensity to trust makes us vulnerable as individuals.'

PROFESSOR RODERICK M KRAMER
'Rethinking Trust',
Harvard Business Review, June 2009

CHAPTER 6

First Date Feels

During another phone call a couple of days later, Max suggested we have dinner together. When I said that sounded nice, he told me he'd choose a place and make a booking. *He'd choose a place AND make the booking?! Swoon.* Today, I can see this was just another way Max liked to maintain control, but at the time, I only saw this as a massive turn-on. Let's be honest – when you're a single working parent who's suffering from decision-making fatigue, finding time for a phone call, let alone a date, can feel like a Herculean mission. It could have been his willingness to handle the plans or the ease of our conversations, but I found myself wanting nothing more than to literally and figuratively don a pair of gladiator sandals and meet up with Max. We made plans for one of my coveted kid-free Wednesday nights in mid-May 2016.

For how natural everything had felt between us thus far, I was surprisingly nervous about taking the 'in-person' next step. *What if he doesn't like me? What if I don't like him? What if I get salad stuck in my teeth? What if he gets broccoli in his? Do I tell him? Would I want him to tell me? What if the banter doesn't translate to real life? What if we run out of things to talk about? What do I wear? Does he want kids? Why haven't I asked if he wants kids? I wonder how he treats hospitality workers …*

Max: T-5. Can't wait to see you tonight.

He's counting down the hours. Cute.

In an effort to calm my nerves and quiet the cacophony of thoughts ringing in my head before our date, I went for a post-work drink with a colleague while Max drove into the city to pick me up. Just as I'd hoped, the preliminary gin and tonic worked a treat and I managed to transform back into my 'cool and casual' self by the time he texted to tell me he was waiting in his car. *He's early.*

Max: Side lane, navy RR, here when you're ready.

The truth is, the gin and catch-up with my friend was feeling so good that I had actually ordered a second round only a minute before Max texted. Upon explaining my little liquid-courage conundrum to Max, I asked if he'd like to come in for a quick drink and to meet my friend.

Max: I'm parked in a no-stopping zone.
Tracy: That's okay. There's heaps of parking nearby.

Max: Look, if you don't want to leave yet, I'll just meet you at the restaurant. Or we can find another time to have dinner.

It's always hard to judge someone's tone in a text but Max's last response gave me the sense that he was getting the shits. Not wanting to get off on the wrong foot and feeling rude that I'd switched up the plan, I assured him I'd be out in a minute. With that, I abandoned my drink, said goodbye to my friend and headed for the door. In the seconds it took to get outside, I tried to picture what Max would look like in person. Up until this point, I'd only seen a carefully curated collection of photos from his online dating profile. There was the 'I Run Marathons with My Eight-Pack on Show' pic, the 'I'm a Laidback Local Who Knows Where to Get the Best Coffee in NYC' pic, the 'Sand in My Hair, Don't Care' pic, the 'Look at This [obscure C-List] Celeb I Met' pic and, last but not least, the 'Oh, This Old Blazer, Crew-neck and Loafer Look?' pic.

Hoping I'd have the same response that I'd had to the gratuitous shirtless marathon-running, abs-for-days pic, I was admittedly underwhelmed when I got into Max's 'navy RR' and took a sneaky scan of him before leaning over and giving him the obligatory kiss on the cheek hello. Even though Max still looked fit, athletic and like someone who'd have defined abdominal muscles south of their bellybutton (you know the 'V' I'm talking about), he was thicker and shorter than I anticipated. Let's just say he was more boxer in the dating app and more bulldog in real life. What was accurate was his blindingly blond hair, Colgate-commercial-worthy smile and startling blue eyes.

No joke, they were like *National Geographic* award-winning portrait eyes.

While I'm sure Max was playing the same mental 'expectations vs reality' comparison game in his head about me, we made our way to a restaurant called Ms. G's in Potts Point. Whatever weird tension I'd felt over the phone must have dissipated because Max was happily asking me about the friend I'd met up with and how my work day went. As I was beginning to tell him about the virtual reality project eBay had me working on, Max whipped into a no-parking zone directly in front of the restaurant. Knowing he'd get a fine, I suggested we find another parking spot.

'It'll only be a hundred dollars. I'll just pay it,' Max said with a cheeky grin before turning off the ignition and opening his door. Weird, seeing as he wouldn't stay in the no-parking zone so I could finish my drink …

I couldn't decide if he was just *very* eager to start our date or was low-key trying to show me that he was a money's-no-object kind of guy. Because I had silently judged him for referring to his car as 'RR', I was keeping my fingers crossed that it was the former. (By the way, if you put 'RR' into Google Translate and put the settings from Douchebag to English, it translates to 'Range Rover'.)

Once settled at our table, we ordered wine and an entrée of prawn toast. To ease the awkwardness of not having anything to consume or do with our hands, I started asking Max about his work.

'So, sixteen years in New York? That's a long time to live overseas.'

'Yeah, I never anticipated that I'd stay away that long.

At first, I just went because I got a scholarship to MIT but that led to an internship at Lockheed Martin. Due to funding cuts by the Clinton administration, I took a job at J.P. Morgan.'

'How'd you get a scholarship to MIT?'

'I've always been pretty good at maths but when I was sixteen, some people came in and did testing and said I could be a member of Mensa. I didn't want to take the title but having the results that I did kind of snowballed interest in me being sent overseas to study on scholarship.'

Full confession – the only reason I know what Mensa is is because I read in some celebrity gossip article that Geena Davis is a member.

'Clearly, you're a numbers guy …'

'You could say that,' Max laughed.

'Lockheed Martin – that's an aerospace company, right?'

'That's right. I was working on algorithms that assisted NASA with shuttle launches. There was also a weird stint where I worked as an advisor to the United States Treasury. I admit, that was a bit of a *Forrest Gump* time in my life. Every time I'd rock up to 1500 Pennsylvania Avenue, I thought about how random the whole thing was.'

'You know, I had the same thought when I worked at a sausage crumbing factory on the Gold Coast.'

Max nearly snort-laughed. 'You worked at a sausage factory?'

'Some girls fold jeans at Sportsgirl after school, others throw sausages on a conveyor belt.'

Max's wide eyes and smile told me he was clearly amused by my former factory life.

'I have such a funny image of you in my head right now.'

'The worst part was once the sausages had been crumbed, they'd go through for a second pass and I would have to gently rub the excess crumb off.'

'You were a sausage wanker,' Max joked.

'And yet somehow, I wasn't bullied in school.'

⚑

Mensa? MIT? NASA? The United States Treasury? Sure, it all sounded a bit fantastical but there are actual people working in these fields … Why not Max Tavita? And more importantly, why would he lie?

⚑

Our waiter delivered the wine and prawn toast. After taking a sip of a beautiful riesling, I asked, 'And when did you sell your soul to Wall Street again? Before playing professional ping pong or after hopping on a shrimp trawler?'

'I know, it sounds ridiculous, doesn't it? Just as the internship with Lockheed was losing funding I was conveniently poached by Wall Street to write and develop code for a new technology that would enable high-frequency trades.'

Before I could respond, Max kissed his hand, raised it to the sky and added, 'Thank you, royalties!'

For some reason, even with all the IQ and money talk, Max didn't come off as pretentious. If anything, he felt a bit like a 'mathlete' meets 'science club member' meets 'collector'. Why did this matter to me? For starters, I wasn't interested in dating a wanker. (Crumbed sausage wankers –

yes. Superficial stockbrokers – no.) Secondly, the term 'generational wealth' hasn't sat well with me since my time volunteering in India. To be clear, I'm not anti-capitalism and anti-owning nice things. I have already admitted that ashram life is not for me. I'm just not overly impressed with fortune, fame and people who casually use 'high-net-worth individual' in a sentence.

Evidently, Max was not impressed with any type of food one could describe as 'gooey'. When we'd been deciding what to order, Max had made it clear he couldn't do soft textures. Guacamole? No, thank you. Aioli? Can't. Burrata? Absolutely not. It was hard for me to empathise with his discriminative eating habits, but they weren't a deal-breaker. After all, you couldn't pay me enough to eat lamb brains or sheep liver. And the more we spoke about the food, the more I understood just how seriously Max took his health, even when he wasn't in training mode for a triathlon. Although I was impressed with his knowledge on the subject, Max must have noticed my eyes start to glaze over during his man-ologue on intermittent fasting, because he shifted the conversation toward me. He wanted to know more about my virtual reality project.

'eBay may not be sending people to outer space but what we're doing is pretty incredible,' I said. I explained that we'd teamed up with Myer to create the world's first virtual reality department store. Max made the right noises and looked genuinely interested so I went into some detail about how customers would wear special VR glasses, which we were calling 'shopticals', and would browse, select and add items to their cart with their eyes. 'Shopping with your eyes. Who would have thought?'

'Oh, like a virtual mind map,' he said. 'The British spy inside me loves this idea.'

'It's cool, isn't it? After spending the last fifteen years on traditional corporate ad campaigns, it's been a welcome change. Can't believe the launch event is in less than a week.'

Because this very project got me up at 4.30 am and had me burning the candle at both ends, nothing could contain the yawn that escaped from my mouth. In my past life, this yawn may have been met with, 'Seriously? You can't make it past 8.30 pm?' But Max looked at me sympathetically and offered to get me home. For the first time in a *long* time, this simple gesture felt like someone was looking after me and had my best interests at heart. Thinking I'd just grab an Uber, I was surprised when Max said he'd drive me to a taxi rank in Woolloomooloo. After he explained it was on his way home, I accepted the offer and got back into his car, which, by the way, did *not* have a parking ticket.

As far as first dates in your forties go, this one felt like a success. No, it hadn't gone on for hours, but the conversation continuously flowed and our interest in each other felt genuine. There was just one last obligatory first to navigate: the goodbye. I was confident we could manage a solid hug, but there was one question I didn't know the answer to: *would he go in for a kiss?*

Max parked opposite the taxi rank. On our walk over, he pointed to an apartment on the wharf. 'I used to live there.'

Woolloomooloo Finger Wharf apartments are seriously expensive … like, only-celebrities-and-mining-tycoons-can-afford-them type of expensive. The first words that came to my mind were, *Fuck off!* Thankfully, the only words that came out of my mouth were, 'Was your neighbour Russell Crowe?'

Max's blue eyes glimmered as he described his exclusive views of Sydney Harbour. I couldn't help but wonder, *Is he peacocking right now?* Before I had time to figure out the answer, the bright headlights of a taxi pulled our focus from grandeur to goodbyes. Max and I locked eyes. After a brief pause, he placed a kiss – not a peck – on my cheek before opening the car door.

On my ride back to Freshwater, I thought about how much I'd like to see Max again. Sure, there were a few quirks here and there, but mostly I just saw a guy who'd lived the Sydney high life, the New York and London banking life, and was now looking for the simple life. Simple felt good.

For how quickly I collapsed into bed, it was interesting to see how fast my fingers reached for my phone. Everything that had come out of his mouth had been the perfect combination of flirty, interesting, caring and insightful. Leaving him kind of felt like I'd just finished a carton of fries from McDonald's … satisfying, but I still needed to do one final dive into the bag to see if I could get a bit more. Enter social media. I typed in 'Max Tavita' on Instagram. *Nothing.* Facebook. *Nothing.* LinkedIn. *Nothing.* Too tired to plunge into the internet rabbit hole, I chucked my phone on the bedside table and went to sleep.

CHAPTER 7

Fancy a Cuppa?

Less than a week later, Max and I found ourselves on date number two. Instead of wine in Potts Point, we were having chai in Circular Quay. I'd been working onsite for the eBay virtual reality department store event when Max asked if I wanted to meet up for a quick cuppa after his meeting in the city. Seeing as I'd been experiencing the near-hourly adrenaline surges that come with planning and promoting such a large event, my body instantly relaxed at the thought of a warm mug in my hands.

I arrived at the cafe about five minutes before Max and ordered a chai latte for me and a ristretto with a side of mineral water for Max before taking a seat at a table. When Max walked in, I took note of how casual he looked in a white t-shirt and black drop-crotch canvas pants. I also noticed he looked a bit uncomfortable because he kept pulling his slightly-too-tight shirt away from his tummy. He spotted me and walked over. I stood to give him a kiss on the cheek.

'Do you mind if we swap seats?' he asked. 'I prefer to sit with my back against the wall.'

⚐

Odd. But then again, I don't like using a toilet unless I've checked for spiders.

⚐

'Sure, but I'll need to know more about this "preference". You didn't mention it in your dating bio,' I said playfully while swapping chairs.

Max cracked a grin. 'I haven't always been like this, I promise. It's just … after 9/11, I'm hyperaware of my surroundings. I need to know where the exits are.'

I did a double take and put the timelines together before blurting out, 'It just occurred to me that you would have been in New York when the towers came down.'

'I was,' Max said in a matter-of-fact way.

Our drinks arrived, which forced me to make small talk with the waiter before I could ask my next question. 'I feel like everyone intricately remembers where we were when we heard a plane had crashed into the first tower. Where were you?'

Max nodded. 'Pretty close actually. I was less than a block away from the towers when the first plane hit. I was with a mate I used to work with. Guy named Peter.'

My eyes widened and my gaze became even more intense.

Max leaned forward. 'It was surreal. Nothing looked, sounded, smelled or felt the same. It was full-on chaos because we all knew we needed to get out of wherever we were but we also didn't know where to go. I've never been so disoriented.'

'Were you hurt?'

'Thankfully, no. We ran. Mostly, I was in disbelief. My eyes burned from the dust and my ears throbbed from the loud blasts but no major injuries.' Max took a sip of his ristretto and pulled his shirt off his belly again before adding, 'I can't unhear the sounds.' He went on to do impressions of what the plane sounded like hitting the building, before describing how the building and people running both moaned and wailed.

Max looked away. 'But the worst were the screams. I still hear the screams the most.'

'I can't imagine how traumatising that must have been for you. I was at my apartment watching the towers come down on TV and I still get flashbacks to how horrible it was. Was your friend okay? Peter?'

'Yeah, Peter was fine. But the worst part was that we'd been waiting for a friend who worked on the twenty-sixth floor of the first tower. Sal. She was thirty-four and just about to get married. We used to work with her.'

I was at a loss for words. Max went on for a few more minutes describing in detail the other people he knew who had lost their lives that day. He must have been significantly impacted because he spoke about each of them so clearly. First and last names, ages, which companies they worked for, which division they were in, as well as which floor they were on when the planes hit.

At some point, I reached for Max's hand. 'This is absolutely heartbreaking.'

Max took a deep breath. 'Yeah. It fucked me up real good there for a while. I actually had to take a leave of absence from work. Most people in the industry did.'

'Did you come back to Australia?'

'No, I moved to Italy and ended up competing in triathlons. Anything work-related triggered flashbacks so I pretty much did nothing but swim, bike and run.' Max grinned. 'I also managed a few nice meals in Lake Como and a boat trip or two on the Adriatic Sea. It was just what I needed at the time to deal with it all.'

'I totally get why you'd need to get away after that. I did a similar thing with India after my dad died.' I wished I had more time to keep hearing about how Max had overcome such a horrific experience but glancing at my watch, I saw that I needed to go. 'I hate cutting this short, but I need to get back to my reality of virtual reality. Thanks for meeting me for a cuppa.'

Max straightened in his chair. 'I feel so bad. We've spoken so much about me today. I haven't asked you any questions.'

'That's okay. Max, what you've experienced is huge. Thanks for sharing it with me.'

Max stood and gave me a hug. 'Thanks for listening. And thanks for making time for me. I know you're under the pump at work.'

'You're the perfect amount of distraction,' I said.

Just as I was about to leave, I stopped and asked Max if he wanted to come and check out the eBay exhibition.

Max pursed his lips and then answered, 'No, because if I come, I'll want to invest.'

I laughed and gave him a little tap on the arm. 'Good one, jerk.'

On my way back to work, I had a noticeable pep to my step because Max really was the perfect amount of distraction. Sure, his off-handed comments about how much money he had made him a jerk from time to time but there were so many more pros. Consistent and charming, he was exactly the type of person I wanted to date while trying to rebuild my life after divorce.

According to the Australian Department of Foreign Affairs and Trade, there were 15,000 Australians living in New York City in 2001. Did I find it hard to believe that Max could have been one of them? Absolutely not. Did I consider that Max was strategically telling me this sob story in an effort to gain my sympathy and trust? Also no.

CHAPTER 8

Bonding in Bondi

For a single working parent who felt like the walking definition of time-poor, it was amusing to see just how much time I could come up with for Max. Sure, I had to let go of the concept of alone time, but that was fine if it meant getting to see the guy who always brightened my day. For the next two months, we managed to see each other about once a week and every other weekend. Of course, we spoke multiple times every day. Neither of us had outright said it, but it was clear we were heading into sleepover territory.

As I walked up to Max's Bondi apartment for the first time in early June, I noted the modern and angular facade of 1 Jaques Avenue. Inside, the apartment was just as clinical. Everything was either grey, white or a blue-veined marble. And unlike the other beachside apartments I've walked into over the years, there was not a speck of sand anywhere. Honestly, it was as clean as a hospital room. Knowing how much Max liked to surf, I found this odd. While giving me a little tour, Max explained that his surfboards and wetsuits lived on his balcony and he always used the building's outdoor shower before entering his apartment after a surf or run. *Okay, so he's a clean freak.*

Originally, we had planned to grab dinner in the city after work because it was my kid-free Wednesday and our weekly date night. However, it was freezing outside and the State of Origin happened to be on, so I suggested we grab some beers and takeaway from China Diner and hang at his place. When we got back with the food, I started dishing it up on the kitchen bench because Max's dining table was in no condition for eating. Instead of a glass bowl of fresh fruit or some other standard centrepiece, Max had a bank of monitors on the table which made it feel like Bloomberg was third-wheeling our date. Even though Max did most of his work from an office in the city, he said he needed to be able to work through the night, hence the at-home set-up.

Max and I sat next to each other on his black leather lounge to eat our food and watch the game. Worried I'd get sauce on the Hermès throw that was draped over the arm, I moved it to a nearby chair before diving into my Kung Pao chicken. When New South Wales was up 4–2, my phone dinged. Feeling terrible for texting during our date, I explained that my brothers, Mum and I always have a bit of a digital cheer party for Queensland. We celebrate the wins, curse the losses, talk about which players are playing well and which ones need to pull their heads in. And, of course, there are often heated words about referees. Max, a Blues fan through and through, waved away my concern and weighed into the banter. Just as I put my phone down, Max's phone rang. I glanced over and saw the name *Ana Terrén* on his screen.

'Sorry, I'm going to have to take this.'

While half-watching the game, I half-listened to Max's conversation. It was impossible not to eavesdrop. His apartment wasn't very big and he paced the length of it as he spoke about what he needed from Ana and someone named Claudia in order to execute the investment strategy they'd agreed on. He kept it brief, hung up and then sat back on the lounge beside me.

'Work call?' I prompted, trying to sound interested but not too interested.

'Yep. Ana is the CEO of the family office and Claudia coordinates the deals. Claudia is still quite new, hence the micromanaging, but Ana and I go back to my J.P. Morgan days. I think we've been working together for close to twenty years now.'

'Did she work with you at J.P.?'

'Yeah, she found her way to Wall Street much earlier than I did and is an absolute gun. We're only five years apart in age but Ana has been a career mentor of mine pretty much since day dot. I wouldn't have taken this role at the family office if she wasn't at the helm.'

I liked hearing that Max considered Ana a mentor. It's always refreshing when someone acknowledges they don't have all the answers. It's even more refreshing to find yourself sitting in comfortable silence with someone. For the next thirty minutes, Max and I were enthralled by the footy and really only came up for air to pass a spring roll or make a verbal jab about each other's team. And then it happened: Queensland scored a try and won the game 6–4. My double-fist-pump into the air may have been a tad over the top but I was ecstatic that we won (and that Max didn't get any gloating rights). Max was smiling and shaking his head at my display of 'the Maroons will always be better than the Blues' when he said something that made my heart skip a beat.

'I have to be honest with you, Trace. I could not be any happier than I am right now. Sitting here with you, drinking a beer, watching the footy – I reckon you're my girl.'

At that moment, I felt the exact same way. The last couple of years had felt like hell but there was no denying how happy I was that it all led me to this point: footy and a beer with someone who was starting to feel more and more like *my guy*. I clasped Max's hand and told him I was starting to suspect he might just be my person. After a few more beats of comfortable silence, Max started reflecting on how we'd both walked such rocky paths but managed to finally find calm.

In those early days of dating, we were always starting and stopping fifty conversations at once. That night, we got onto the topic of his previous engagement. On our first date, Max had told me that he'd never been married but had been engaged and it hadn't worked out. I'd been curious since then but didn't want to seem nosy. Now I felt like I could ask what had happened.

Max let out a long sigh. 'She was a drinker. Liked the wine a bit too much. We were engaged for two years and did tons of therapy but it was never going to change.' He picked up his beer and looked at it before taking the last sip. 'That's one of the reasons why I really don't drink that much. And why I'm still in therapy.'

I frowned and gave him a look of sympathy. 'I'm sorry to hear that.'

'Now that there's been time and space between us – three years – I can see many other reasons why we wouldn't have worked. Different values, different ideas of the future … In a way, I think leaving because of her alcoholism was really just the nudge I needed to get out and find the right person. Lucky we didn't get married.'

'Was she American? Is she still in the US?'

'Aussie actually. Her name's Bec. We met in Australia but she and her kids moved over to New York for a while. It was a bit of a hairy situation because her ex-husband was a nightmare. I think the hardest part about the whole relationship breakdown is how much I miss her boys … as well as her dad. We keep in touch but it's just not the same.'

Max went on to tell me more about Bec and her boys. As he described how he'd started dating her when she was going through her divorce, I could empathise with the stress she must have been feeling.

By now, it was close to 10.30 pm and Max asked if I wanted to stay the night. Admittedly unprepared for a sleepover, I borrowed a t-shirt and a pair of boxer shorts and brushed my teeth with my finger (we were definitely not at the sharing a toothbrush stage) before crawling into bed.

Seeing as Max fell asleep the second his head hit the pillow, I figured sex wasn't on the cards. I don't want this to sound like a humble brag, but this may have been the first time I'd ever gotten in bed with a date, especially after two months, and they hadn't tried it on. Even though I was truly too tired for sex, it was weird to notice how much I still wanted to be wanted. While Max lay next to me in near corpse-like form (on his back, arms crossed on his chest), I ruminated on the reasons why he hadn't tried to have sex with me yet, ran through my list of things to do, second-guessed a good chunk of my life choices and then visualised the next day's meetings before finally catching that glorious wave of sleep.

I woke to the sound of Max's shaver buzzing. My phone said it was 5.34 am and my heavy eyelids concurred. En route to the kitchen for a cup of tea, I gave a sleepy wave to Max, who was nearly free of the light blond stubble on his chin. While the caffeine was doing its thing in my body, I considered catching an Uber back to mine to change clothes but decided I could get away with repeating my outfit from the day before. Plus, I'd snuck in a change of underwear and a fresh top *just in case*. I put my mug down on the bench and went back into Max's room to get dressed. Max was in the process of putting on a navy suit. Up until this point, I'd never seen him all done up. I took a seat on the end of his bed and watched him tuck in a double-cuffed shirt before buckling his belt.

'Can you pass me my cufflinks? They're in that box.' Max gestured to a Cartier box that was sitting on his bedside table.

'Sure.' I reached for the box and took out two classic and perfectly understated platinum cufflinks. Max slipped them into place and went to his closet to grab a pair of freshly polished loafers. While pondering whether he shined his own shoes or was someone who got it done in The Strand,

I stood up and put on my jeans, white tee and blazer, feeling very Country Road to his Cartier. Once Max had his shoes on, he grabbed a wad of cash from what I assumed was his sock drawer and placed it in his wallet. Noting we were both ready to leave, I picked up Max's jacket from the foot of the bed and handed it to him.

'Tom Ford. Nice.'

'I call this my 007 look. Daniel Craig and I lived in the same apartment building in New York actually.'

It was fun to see this version of Max, even if I secretly thought that he looked like a B-grade Daniel Craig. (Sorry, not many can compete.) So far, I'd seen 'down-to-earth jeans and a t-shirt Max' and 'knockabout surfer in Havaianas and a singlet Max'. I won't lie – I was into 'investment banker Max'. Probably because while he looked the part, he still had an Aussie-ness about him. I mean, I wouldn't be the first woman to feel attracted to a well-educated and driven professional who spoke with a slight Aussie twang and spent his weekdays in a Tom Ford suit and his weekends in boardies and singlets …

'Alright, Rascal. Let's get to work.'

I also found it endearing that everyone and everything, including me, got a nickname … or three. So far, I'd been 'Trace', 'T' and 'Rascal'.

After throwing my bag over my shoulder, I asked Max, 'Do you want a coffee? I have a very strong need for an extra hot, extra strong latte right now.'

'I've already had a triple-strength ristretto so I'd better not have more. But I'll take you to Cali Press. They do the best coffee.'

Just before we walked out the door, Max paused at the table in his entry and slipped on the Rolex that was sitting between a Patek Philippe and a Panerai. *So, he likes fancy watches.*

Max spent a good portion of the drive into the city on the phone with Ana. I couldn't hear exactly what Ana was saying because Max had earbuds in, but I could hear her voice from time to time. She sounded warm, smart and very focused as Max relayed plans and investments for his day. Just as Max was wrapping up the conversation, he turned onto O'Connell Street and pulled into a no-parking zone.

'Bub, my office is just up there on Bligh, but I'm going to have to go into the underground car park. Do you want to hop out here? You can walk down Hunter Street to eBay.'

'Sure thing.' I gave him a kiss on the cheek and said we'd chat later.

While walking the rest of the way to work, I thought about how attractive Max had looked in his suit, which made me instantly want to plan our next date. I was kid-free again that Friday, but apparently Fridays were out for him because that's when the US stock market was wrapping up for the week. He'd have to be online. Just then, my phone vibrated.

Max: Fancy a run on Saturday?
Tracy: Definitely.

That night, I opened my journal and found myself writing a letter to Max that I had no intention of sending. For how open and vulnerable we'd been and how intense our connection was becoming, I couldn't help but feel like he was holding back. By journalling 'to Max', I was hoping to discover what obstacles needed to be cleared without having to ask him outright.

Spending time with you last night was awesome. Dinner, chats, watching the footy together. My perfect night. Again, not a lot of physical interaction other than snuggling on the couch which was lovely, but more soon would be good too.

I like the connection I have with you. I find you interesting. I enjoy my time with you and find myself wanting more. Who knows where it will end … or begin. All I know is that I like the time we spend together.

CHAPTER 9

Coach Max

Of course I was intimidated by the idea of running with Max. After all, he was a marathoner and once-upon-a-time professional triathlete who had completed not one but two Ironman races. Do you know what people do in an Ironman? They swim for 3.9 kilometres (in an ocean that is no doubt teeming with sharks), ride a bike for 180 kilometres and *then* run a marathon. That's right – they finish with a 42.2-kilometre jaunt. As someone whose 'all out' run has been compared to the Cliffy Young shuffle, I really had to talk myself into this little run-date with Max.

The plan: we'd leave from mine in Freshwater, head over the stairs at Queenscliff, run down Manly Beach's footpath and turn around at Shelly Beach. Even though my running style and pace were comparable to a 75-year-old's, I was and am a fairly fit person. And so, when Max arrived at 7 am the following Saturday, I laced up my joggers, threw a hat on my head and hit the ground running. I'm not typically a morning person, but the first few minutes felt relatively easy. Max and I were chatting away about the footy, dodging dog walkers and merrily making our way down the stairs to Manly Beach. Just when the run started to feel challenging, we discovered that Manly was packed with tourists and there was no way we'd be achieving sub six-minute kms with that amount of foot traffic. *Slow and steady.* Just the way I liked it.

As we were approaching the beach volleyball nets near North Steyne, Max abruptly suggested we turn around because the footpath was too crowded. Sure, there was an annoying amount of people, but not enough to break my stride. I thought it was very odd and sudden and I would have happily kept going, but I nodded and did an about-turn in the next break of people.

In hindsight, I wonder if he saw someone he knew and got spooked.

'We can go to Curl Curl instead,' Max said.

'Ugh, I didn't anticipate having to run back up the devil stairs so soon,' I said through my panting.

'You can do it!'

Even before we got back to the stairs, the slight incline of Bridge Road was taking its toll on me. My legs felt like sandbags and my heart was pounding. It could have been the fact that the sets of stairs going back to Freshwater really were hectic or the look of death on my face, but Max apparently felt the need to help.

'Come on, T. When it gets really hard and you're really hurting – this is when you need to dig in and push yourself. THIS is where the magic happens and you get stronger and fitter.'

Max's coaching seemed to work because for the first time in the decade that I'd been 'running' the Queenscliff stairs, I found myself at the top without needing to take a break.

'That's it! See, I knew you could do it,' Max said with pride.

Holding back the vomit feeling from the lactic acid coursing through my body, I think I blurted out, 'Fuck going to Curl Curl.'

'Okay, we can save Curl Curl for another day. Want to jump in the ocean?'

YES. Every part of me wanted nothing more than to cool off in the water. After taking our shoes and socks off, I followed Max down the access path to Freshwater Beach, taking note of how bald he actually was. Because Max's hair was so blond and he did such a solid job of combing it over, I hadn't really noticed it before. And god forbid you say something to a man about his receding hairline. About midway to the water, Max dropped his shoes and stripped his shirt off, revealing a rather impressive scar on his left shoulder. When I reached him, I put my shoes down and took off my shirt. Running shorts and a sports bra would make do for swimming.

'What's this from?' I asked, tracing my fingers across Max's back.

'Shark,' Max replied with a cheeky twinkle and half smile.

'What's it really from?'

'The story isn't that exciting … I was stabbed in the subway in New York.'

'No, seriously … What's it from? Melanoma?'

Max laughed. 'I'm not joking. I got stabbed. It was about 3 am and a guy demanded I give him money. I should have just shut up and given him cash or my watch or something, but instead I opened my big mouth. I can't remember what I said but it did not go down well, hence the knife to the back.'

I know, right? Stabbed? On the subway? In New York? Red flag? Look, I was suspicious too. Maybe not suspicious as much as, 'Really? Did that actually happen?' But what was I going to do? Accuse him of lying? Max made a lot of outlandish off-the-cuff comments and jokes, which is why I took to letting them roll off my back. I was probably also so woozy from sprinting up those devil stairs that the only flags I was capable of seeing were in front of the Freshwater Surf Life Saving Club.

Over the next few months, Max and I continued to run together a lot. Thanks to his constant coaching, I found the magic to not only make it back up the Queenscliff stairs but also all the way to Curl Curl. When I stayed with him in Bondi, we did long runs or short sprint sessions through Rose Bay, only slowing down to enjoy the aromas wafting from Catalina restaurant, before continuing along the golf course. On the few occasions I was too worn out for a personal training sesh with 'Coach Max', we opted for walks through Tamarama to Coogee, paddleboarding in Bronte, or my personal favourite, Max's cheat days featuring hot chips and a beer on the grass.

During one of our first park picnics, I munched down on chips while Max nibbled on pieces of biltong. Aside from his sweet tooth that would come out any time he was near a bag of Snakes, I had yet to see him stray from his Paleo ways. Never had I met someone with so much discipline for their diet and exercise habits. In fact, never had I met someone so disciplined in every life area. Unlike myself and almost everyone I know, he never scrolled mindlessly through his phone. Whenever he had downtime, he was running, surfing or reading.

On one hand, I liked that he didn't seem addicted to social media or doomscrolling through news articles. But on the other hand, I felt a bit cheated. Wasn't getting to see your prospective partner posing in questionable 80s attire such as a hypercolour t-shirt or sharing an entire album dedicated to a single night out a rite of passage for people dating in the age of social media? To be fair, I was also a busy girl and wasn't one who spent much time on socials, but at least I had the decency to leave him enough of a digital footprint to know I can pull off both brown and blonde hair.

'How come you're not on social media? Too cool for school?'

Max finished his mouthful of bougie South African jerky and chuckled. 'Not cool enough, T! I just like to keep a low profile. In my line of work, everyone always wants something from you. I also have an issue with letting companies like Facebook profit from my data. Surely, you know that you're the product, Trace.'

'I do know that. But I also appreciate being heavily targeted by ads for exotic holidays.'

Max laughed and elaborated, 'It's kind of like my apartment in Bondi. I wanted something small and understated because the more stuff that people see you have, the more they take advantage of you. I've lived that life and I'm here to tell you, it doesn't make you happy. I'm really just looking for a simple life, T. The ocean, surfing and decent people. Plus, when I got back from New York, my focus was to live in the present moment. I want to be with whatever is actually right in front of me. Like you.'

Cue: a tidal wave of oxytocin.

'I could get used to this present moment,' I said with a wink.

⚑

For as strange as it was to not have any sort of social media in 2016, it wasn't completely foreign to me. In fact, Cath didn't have any social accounts either. Not even LinkedIn. The need to be seen hadn't taken hold of my generation just yet, and Max's line about a simple life was plausible … and charming.

⚑

That night, I opened my journal and wrote to Max. For some reason, I always had so much to say after the fact.

Even though I don't know where this will go and where we will end up, I know it's right. I'm more relaxed about the lack of physical intimacy this week than last. Like me, you like taking things slowly.

I just find it so hard to believe that you don't want more when we're together. Do you hold yourself back or do you just not want it? Whichever way it falls, I enjoy the time we have together. You make me laugh. You make me think. And most of all, you make me feel good.

CHAPTER 10

'The Slow Burn'

I'm not sure if this is universal for all women or just true for my circle of friends, but when casually dating, we tend to give our prospect(s) a nickname for ease of reference. Some of my favourites include, 'The Hot French German', 'Naughty Greg' and 'NBB (Nice But Boring) Accountant'. Nearly three months after our first date, Max earned a nickname I wasn't thrilled about: 'The Slow Burn'. At first, I thought us not heating things up was because my single mum co-parenting schedule, coupled with the fact that I wasn't anywhere near ready to introduce him to Asha, drastically hindered the amount of opportunities we had to hang out. But then I started to notice that even when we did find the time, The Slow Burn wasn't exactly trying to set my physical world on fire.

Let's take our day date to Palm Beach, for example. Max showed up at mine at 11 am and texted that he was waiting out the front. When I walked outside, it took me a moment to find him because he wasn't in his work 'RR'. He also wasn't in his personal 'RR', which I'd recently discovered he owned. Then I spotted his white hair and tanned arm waving from the driver's window of a white ute. I hopped in, gave him a kiss hello and, with wide eyes and a playful 'omg' tone, asked, 'Another car?'

Max explained that he'd wanted to bring paddle boards and knew we'd be wet and sandy, so he'd opted to drive his VW Amarok – aka his 'beach car'. We laughed about the absurdity of having multiple cars in Bondi and how parking was like a game of Tetris.

Due to the unusually sunny and warm weather, we planned to go paddleboarding on Pittwater Bay, grab lunch at the original Boathouse cafe (may she rest in peace) and walk up to Barrenjoey Lighthouse. I couldn't remember the last time I'd been up to Palm Beach. Unless I have a visitor from overseas and am doing the Tour de Sydney circuit, which includes but is not limited to having drinks at Opera Bar, walking under/over the Harbour Bridge, taking copious pictures by Mrs Macquarie's Chair, sweating out a hangover via the Coogee to Bondi walk and brunching at Palm Beach, I never have a good enough reason to venture to the pricey tip of the peninsula. After all, I can overpay for coffee and a good view in Freshwater.

Max tapped me on the shoulder to get my attention. 'I used to live in that house.'

When I looked up, Max was pointing his finger at a beachfront, modern two-storey home on South Curl Curl Beach. 'You did? When?'

'In my twenties. But because I spent most of my time in the States, I ended up renting it out. Sold it a few years ago because I prefer to spend my time in Bondi. Easier to get to the city.'

'It's incredible. What a spectacular spot.'

Max went on to talk about the renovations he'd done and how nice it was to have his ristrettos on the beach at 4 am. 'I do my best thinking when the rest of the world is asleep,' he said.

I smiled and shared that I was more of a night owl but had been working on being a morning person. Not 4 am early (I'm not a lunatic) but 6 am was getting very familiar since becoming a mother.

'If I don't get at least five minutes to make a cup of tea before Asha wakes, I'm not a very nice person.'

Max laughed and put his hand on mine. 'Speaking of Asha. When do you think I'll get to meet her? Have you told her about me?'

'I have, actually. Given our close quarters, it's kind of hard to hide the fact that I've been talking to a man on the phone every night.'

'How did she take it?'

'Good! She's an easygoing kid. Maybe we could FaceTime a few times before we tee up an in-person meeting.'

Max squeezed my hand. 'That sounds like a great plan.'

Much to my delight, he didn't let go for the rest of the car ride. Not to sound audacious, but I don't think Nora Ephron could have written a more perfect date. From the moment Max parked (legally) in Palm Beach, everything we did made me feel like I was in a rom-com. There were playful splashes in the water with our paddles, more hand-holding, cuddles with the many designer dogs that ran lead-free and the perfect amount of comfortable silences. For how much we'd crammed into the day, I was surprisingly still full of energy when Max and I reached the lighthouse. After taking a seat on a rock together, Max stared at the ocean, deep in thought.

'If I ever get married, I want it to be here,' Max said.

For a brief moment, I had a pang of sadness remembering my own wedding and how happy I had once been. 'Why Barrenjoey? Aside from the terrible view...'

Max cracked a soft smile, like he was remembering something fondly. 'After my parents died, we scattered their ashes here. It's where I feel closest to them.'

You might think this story sounds like a red flag, but I thought it sounded like one I could relate to. During one of our earlier conversations, I'd confided in Max about the void and sadness I had felt because my dad hadn't been able to walk me down the aisle at my wedding. I know what it's like to search for signs and any sort of connection to a loved one who has left before you were ready. However, with the gift of hindsight, I'd dare say Max used this particular story to continue gaining my sympathy and trust.

Unsure of how deep Max wanted to go, I lightened things up a bit.

'God, it would be hard to get all the guests up here.'

'Yeah, I've got this vision of me getting flown in by a chopper,' Max said with a grin.

I laughed and nudged him. 'Jerk.'

Max laughed and then grew silent as he quietly peered out across the ocean. As I watched him watch nothing in particular, I genuinely thought that we both might start crying. But just as the melancholic energy began to reach boiling point, Max wrapped his arm around me like a teammate on a footy field. 'You're not wrong about that, TT. I'm a total jerk.'

And just like that, Max avoided his emotions and I had yet another nickname. Before I had the chance to even attempt to melt into this little side hug, Max was up and suggesting we make a move. 'How about we head down before the sun sets and grab a couple of beers and snacks? I have a big towel rug we can lie on to watch the moon rise at Avalon Headland.'

'Sure,' I said cheerfully. Internally, I was wondering why he didn't want to stay put in each other's arms … Was he playing a game? Perhaps he thought the age-old equation of *Marriage Talk + Sob Story + Playing Hard to Get = Keen Chick* was going to work on me. Didn't he know I just wanted someone to be still with at Barrenjoey Lighthouse?

Before heading south, Max stopped briefly at the Palm Beach Wine Co, a gorgeous deli and bottle shop, to pick up cheese, crackers and a few Coronas. Once in Avalon, we grabbed the towel from the back of Max's ute before finding the perfect spot to watch the moon rise. Max used his Leatherman to slice the cheese but was, unfortunately, doing a hack job of it.

'Why do I find this so attractive?' I asked flirtatiously.

'Because you're a scout at heart,' Max suggested.

'Possibly. It's like I'm on a date with Bear Grylls. But I must say that cheese looks like it's getting the better of you.'

Max's face lit up at the thought of being compared to one of the world's most capable men. 'I love a girl who isn't all fluffy.'

'I'll take that as a compliment,' I said, reaching for a cracker that Max had already loaded with a pile of cheddar.

Before either of us could talk more shit, we saw the moon poke its head out of the ocean. It wasn't due to be full for two more days but it looked and felt like it was. It was the type of moon that commands your entire presence. Silently, Max and I watched as it lit up the sky, strobed on the waves and provided just enough light that we could still see each other's eyes. For the first time all day, I finally felt the chill of winter. Max wrapped his arm around me and pulled me in close to his body. 'Come over here,' he said.

I smiled and nestled into his nook and instantly felt soothed by the warmth our bodies were creating. *Surely, he can feel it too.* From time to time, I'd switch my gaze from the moon to his face. Half of me was mesmerised by him and the other half was hoping he'd lean in for a kiss. The moon was hanging high in the sky but sadly, I was left feeling low. This cuddle felt more intimate than the footy hug at the lighthouse but I could tell something was holding Max back from fully letting me in. *Maybe he's nervous.*

'I think I might turn into a literal ice cube if we stay out here much longer. Do you want to come back to mine?' I asked.

'That temperature certainly dropped. Yes, let's go to yours.'

When we drove into Freshwater, I asked Max if he wanted to grab a bottle of wine, thinking it might help him relax. He said that sounded nice and volunteered to run into my local bottle shop. Much to my surprise, he came out with a bottle in each hand.

'I couldn't decide which one. I know this is a good year for McLaren Vale shiraz but I like the embossment and colour palette on this label.'

Okay, Patrick Bateman.

Once in my apartment, I changed into less sandy clothes and poured two glasses from the more aesthetically pleasing bottle because I'm also a sucker for a heavy paper weight and nice typesetting.

Max, who'd taken a seat on my lounge, reminded me that he was allergic to my cat, Gracie. 'My nose has become Niagara Falls.'

I picked up our glasses in my right hand and plucked a few tissues for Max with my left before walking over to him.

'I'm so sorry. I admit that owning a cat has not been one of my best life choices.' (Side note: I love Gracie but after she attempted to remove my left cornea with her litter-coated claws for no apparent reason, I've been wishing her a speedy yet peaceful departure.)

'As far as cats go, she's pretty cute but there's no denying that I'm a dog person. Have I told you about my dog, Patch?' Max said.

'No. Was it a Jack Russell? I feel like everyone names their Jack Russell "Patch".'

Max laughed. 'Patch was a mix of everything. His willingness to eat literally anything made me think he was mostly black labrador.' Max paused before continuing with his story. 'After 9/11 happened and I took that leave of absence in Italy, I ended up coming back here briefly. I don't know what compelled me, but I rescued Patch and spent the better part of six months road-tripping across Australia with just him and a rifle. When J.P. Morgan tried to convince me to work remotely with satellite wi-fi, I figured I should just go back to New York. Surprisingly, I didn't own a car that could fit three monitors.'

⚑

I know. Max's story sounds very *Wall Street* meets *Red Dog*, doesn't it? Again, it was hard to know if he was joking or not so I just kind of breezed past it.

⚑

'New York, Italy and the Outback … you must be exhausted.'

Max smiled and gave me a slow nod. 'You can see why I now have the social life of an eighty-year-old, right?'

'I can.'

What I couldn't see was why Max wasn't trying to be more snuggly. I thought about taking things into my own hands but got distracted by how red his eyes had become from spending two minutes with Gracie's tail in his face. Hoping his sex drive would act as an antihistamine, I was disappointed when he placed his wine down after one sip and said he should probably head home.

'Don't you want your wine?'

'I really shouldn't … I have an early start tomorrow and need to drive home. I'm sorry. I shouldn't have said yes to the wine.'

Max stood up and walked to my front door. I followed, worried I wasn't doing a good job of not looking too disappointed and upset. After a quick hug and peck on the cheek, Max was out the door and I was alone with my thoughts. Confused, I grabbed my journal and started writing to him.

> *I get you have 'stuff'. We all do. I'm cool to be patient with you but you gotta throw me a bone, dude. Am I in the friend zone? This is pushing all my buttons right now. I'm trying not to let it get in the way but it's not easy. I need to know you want to be with me. I need to know that you find me attractive. I need to know that you want to touch me, hold my hand, stroke my hair. Anything. Not even sex. Just affection. Closeness. I want to feel close to you on more than a mental and verbal level.*

When I was done, I swapped my journal for my phone and went straight to Google. Surely there had to be something about his parents' plane crash. *Nothing.*

CHAPTER 11

It's More Common Than You Think

Although Max had some sort of guard up, he was undeniably interested in being part of my life. Wednesday night dinners became a weekly occurrence as did lunch on my work-from-home Fridays. The food wasn't gooey but the feelings bubbling inside me were appearing that way. With each interaction, I kept noticing an admittedly unfamiliar feeling that I'd met someone I could talk to about anything. As a (not healthy) form of self-preservation throughout my life, I had frequently turned my emotions off, ignored my intuition or shut down completely. When someone once accused me of being an 'emotional desert', they weren't wrong.

Thinking it would take years to a) do the deep work needed to recultivate the self-love and respect I'd lost, and b) find someone who was willing to have the conversations necessary to form a relationship built on honesty, authenticity and trust, it was borderline intoxicating to discover how vulnerable Max and I could be with each other. It didn't matter if we were talking about our experiences living and working overseas, the breakdowns of former relationships, the loss of loved ones or discussing something as trivial as the many reasons why chicken salt is a non-negotiable add-on for takeaway chips, Max's questions and responses always felt like the perfect combination of compassionate and challenging. There was no denying that this emotional foreplay was making me an emotional oasis, and yet, I couldn't find the confidence to say any of the things I'd been writing in my journal out loud.

Like any warm-blooded female in a 'slow burn' situation, I took Max's lack of physical intimacy as a personal rejection and started questioning myself. *Is it my body? My age? That stray nipple hair?? Do I have halitosis and nobody's bothered to tell me? Maybe he has more than one 'Tracy' to choose from? Perhaps he's having his needs met elsewhere on a Friday night?* As much as I wanted to lean on my friends, I was embarrassed to share the full extent of just how little action there had actually been. When they asked how the sex was, I'd give them a 'meh' and joked that it's all just a bit different in your forties. Plus, I was enjoying the giddiness of a new relationship and didn't want to skip to the part where we complain about body aches and bowel movements. On the few occasions with friends when I did express a lack of self-confidence in the relationship, I was met with the obligatory, 'Trace, you're gorgeous! Who wouldn't want to rip your clothes off?' As kind as it was for them to try and build me up, I always silently answered that question with *Max Tavita*.

For the most part, the intense emotional intimacy counteracted the lack of physical intimacy. Still, I didn't think it would hurt to bring the issue to my therapist just in case. Because none of us were monogamous when it comes to our mental health professionals, my friends and I also gave our therapists nicknames for ease of reference. Knowing I wanted a female perspective, I opted for Bertie and Beth. Why two names? Well, this therapist was a package deal that came with an emotional support dog who curled up at your feet while you divulged your deepest darkest secrets. Funny thing is – Bertie was the therapist and Beth was the dog.

Upon arriving at my session, I slipped off my shoes, took a seat on a well-worn velvet lounge and nestled into a cross-legged position. Beth jumped up and made a nest between my legs as I began to tell Bertie about how I'd met Max and all the things I liked about him. Judging by her soft smile and wide eyes when I described his love of the ocean, dedication to fitness, respect for his health, ability to articulate his feelings and our shared desire for a simple life of sunshine, soul-soothing life chats and quiet nights watching the moon rise out of the ocean, I could tell she was thinking what I was thinking: *so many green flags!*

'There's just one thing,' I added. 'He hasn't tried to have sex with me yet. He's touchy-feely-ish, affectionate and emotionally intimate, but whenever there's been an opportunity for physical intimacy, nothing happens. If anything, he gets awkward and it feels like he's avoiding it.'

'Avoiding it, how?'

'Two nights ago, for example. We had dinner out and went back to my place for a glass of wine. When we were cuddling on the lounge, I attempted to wriggle my way into his nook. This couldn't have been more "I'm keen" body language, right? But instead of pulling me closer, Max pulled back and said he had an upset stomach from something he must have eaten.'

Bertie gave a look of sympathy. 'Did you have frozen yoghurt for dessert? If yes, he could be telling the truth. That stuff can be dodgy at the best of times.'

No joke, Beth looked up at me with a face that confirmed Bertie's fro-yo wisdom. I briefly laughed but this really wasn't a joking matter. Clearly, she needed more evidence. 'Okay, but after another situation nearly identical to that, Max pulled away and said he needed to get home to bed because he had an early morning. Why didn't he just want to sleep in my bed? I've slept at his place numerous times and had to do the early morning dash home. Honestly, it's like he's not that interested in sex … if at all.'

Bertie adjusted herself in her chair. 'You know, Tracy, this is actually way more common than you think, especially for men in their forties. I cannot tell you how many women have sat right where you are and expressed concern that their boyfriend or husband doesn't want to have sex with them. The truth is, not every man has a high sex drive. That doesn't mean that the intimacy isn't there.'

I paused to consider this. Sure, I had long-time married friends who'd shared that they have sex every six months or even every two years, but I was only three months into a new relationship. We should be peaking, right? Could I get used to not being 'sought after' at all times? As annoying as it could sometimes be to get poked in the back at 5 am, it was nice to feel desired. But then again, the 'too much and too often' people had also landed many of my friends in Bertie and Beth's company. I must have been pausing a bit too long because Bertie added, 'No relationship is perfect. We all have to make compromises. The key is that both parties are willing to have open and honest conversations and really listen to what the other person is saying.'

'All Max does is listen,' I joked.

'You've been through so much over the last two years and have finally found a period of peace and calm for you and your daughter. For now, I wouldn't read into the lack of sex. Just focus on building the relationship slowly.'

I took a deep breath and began scratching Beth behind the ears before nodding in agreement. Bertie was right. Regardless of whether Max had low testosterone or just wasn't ready to go to third (or even second) base yet, he was there for me in a million ways I'd never experienced before. And let's be honest, I had also arrived in the relationship with more baggage than a Qantas flight.

That night, I turned to my journal and wrote the words I hoped I could one day say to Max.

Things with you feel different. Different in the sense that I feel like you truly 'get' me. Sometimes, I even feel like you're the male version of me. (But obviously much better at maths and way more successful.) If not the male version of me, you're like my twin soul. I don't know if you believe in that stuff but I do and it's strange, interesting, exhilarating and scary all at the same time. I believe you have it in you. I also believe it's guarded. Believe me — I know that 'guarded' feeling intimately.

I wish there was more time. More time to get to know you. More time to talk, more time to see each other. And then I catch myself and realise that it doesn't all have to happen straight away. You are my slow burn. And I like that it's unfolding slowly. And surely.

CHAPTER 12

Riding the Wave

In early July, Mum came to visit Asha and me in Freshwater. For the first few days she was in town, Max was trading through the night and sleeping during the day. For the rest of the time, he had a terrible tummy bug that kept him hostage in his bathroom. While I was disappointed they didn't get to meet, I was also bummed that I hadn't been able to spend more time with Max before his upcoming work trip to Singapore. On the morning I was due to drop Mum at the airport, I sent Max a quick text to check in on him. I was keeping all limbs crossed that he was better because I *really* wanted to see him before his flight the next day.

Tracy: How are you, Sick Boy?

Max: Just woke up ... dehydrated. Have stopped vomiting but too scared to eat still ...

Tracy: You poor thing. Dry toast?

Max: Hmmmmmmm ok

Tracy: Are you on video meetings this morning? If so, maybe don't risk it. If not, could be worth a try?

By the time I'd hugged Mum goodbye and found my way out of the funhouse they call Sydney airport's car park, a solid hour had passed since I'd sent my last text and I hadn't heard back from Max. Part worried he'd gone south again and part wanting to do something nice for him, I picked up a few soups and herbal tea for him at the supermarket and drove to his apartment. On my way in, I saw a large stack of letters poking out of his never-locked mailbox, all addressed to 'Max Tavita' and looking semi-important. I slipped them under my arm and knocked on Max's door. *Poor guy must have stayed inside all week.*

Max opened the door and asked (quite rudely!), 'What are you doing here?'

'I brought you ginger tea and soup for your tummy. And I got your mail!' The way Max took the bag and letters out of my hands while keeping the door cracked made me feel like an Uber Eats driver. 'Can I come in for a little bit? I can't believe you're off to Singapore tomorrow.'

Max hesitated before opening the door. 'Sure. Yeah. I'm just still sick.'

I smiled and joked, 'That's okay. I just did four years of daycare immunity training. I've had enough gastro to last me a lifetime.'

When I walked into Max's apartment, I couldn't help but notice how little it looked like he was sick. No unmade bed, no packets of Saladas on the bench, no questionable smells … And aside from an empty suitcase that was sitting on the bed, it did not look like he was someone who was about to go on a trip. In fact, he looked happy, healthy and in work-from-home mode as he put the soup I brought into the fridge.

'Thanks for dropping this off but I'm not really up for company. I still need to pack for Singapore and have yet to even attempt toast.'

Sensing that Max really didn't want me there, I nodded and told him that I hoped he would get better and headed to the front door.

'I'll message you later,' Max said.

Before walking out, I paused, waiting for a hug or a kiss. After all, he was about to fly overseas. I got nothing.

The whole way home, I replayed our interaction over and over again. *Why did that feel so uncomfortable?* I was tempted to ask Max what was really going on, but he never messaged and I was trying to not appear needy. Unable to contain my emotions, I opened my journal and let it all pour out.

Dropping in on you today was a stupid idea. And it made me feel like shit. I know you weren't well but I felt completely unwelcome and out of place there today. It was like you didn't appreciate my gesture at all. I brought you tea and soup, which I thought was a nice thing to do but you pretty much dismissed it all. All I wanted to do was let you know I wanted to make sure you were okay and take care of you. I left feeling like shit.

I feel like I'm constantly being pushed away.

By morning, my self-restraint was gone and I had no problem appearing needy. I sent a text asking how he was.

Max: Still sick. Postponing Singapore by a day.
Tracy: Fingers crossed one more good sleep will be the cure.

Miraculously, sleep did seem to be the cure. Before I knew it, Max had landed in Singapore and was sending me loads of updates about his meetings, meals and musings on Confucianism. By the time he was back in Australia and we resumed our weekly Wednesday dinner dates, I had chalked up his rudeness to being hangry and stressed. Even though things still weren't progressing physically per se, I was happy to see that we were discovering even more ways to connect.

•

It feels sacrilegious writing this because I've lived within walking distance of multiple world-class surf breaks for a good portion of my life, but I didn't learn how to surf properly until 2016. In my defence, I'd spent the majority of my youth on a hockey field and my twenties working sixteen-hour days. And by the time I hit my thirties and became a mum, the only thing I felt capable of riding were the waves of toddler emotions. When I confessed this to Max a week after he returned from Singapore, he excitedly said, 'I'll push you on some waves, Rascal!'

Within forty-eight hours, Max was at my front door holding a brand-new women's wetsuit.

'Lessons start now,' he said with a grin.

Technically, this was a work-from-home day for me, but it was just before 12 pm and I was due for a lunch break. I reluctantly reached for the wetsuit. 'I've only got an hour … Do I really need the whole costume?'

'Bub, it's the middle of winter. You're going to want to wear this. It's one of the best.'

Confident I was going to look more dolphin emoji than Layne Beachley, I delayed putting it on until we got to the beach. While Max unloaded the 8-foot 'foamie' he'd also bought for me to learn on, I pulled the tags off the wetsuit and began the process of putting it on. And a process it was indeed. Due to it being just slightly too small, it took a fair amount of contorting and a few of those squat-hops to get it up, but somehow I was suited up and ready to get in the water.

Max looked me up and down. 'Now, there's my girl!'

I blushed and thought about how happy I was that Max genuinely wanted to teach me how to surf. 'Alright, give me the board. I can't just wear the outfit,' I said playfully.

'I'll carry it down,' Max offered.

'No, no – this Johnny Utah carries her own board.' *Or does she* … When I tried to pick up the board, I was surprised by how hard it was to manoeuvre even out of the water. As someone who has to really poof her hair up to scrape past the 5-foot mark, it felt like I was trying to carry the trunk of a sequoia tree. It must have looked every bit as painful as it felt because Max took over almost instantly. Once by the water's edge, he placed the board down and went over the basics of how to lie on the board, paddle, 'pop up' and stay up.

'Easy peasy. Alright, let's do this!' I said enthusiastically.

Okay, so surfing is *way harder* than you think it's going to be. It could have been the fact that the board Max got me was a complete beast (I imagine it was like watching Thumbelina try to use a door as a surfboard). Or that I was learning in choppy conditions. But if Max wasn't holding the board and helping me sling my body onto it, I really struggled. With that being said – I loved it and started making surfing a weekly thing. Right-sized board and optimal conditions or not, surfing is one of the best mindfulness activities because it demands your full presence while simultaneously delivering cold water therapy. There are a lot of things you could think about while in the ocean: sharks, other surfers, lightning, your grocery list, jellyfish or, the most terrifying of all – seaweed touching your leg. But the moment you let your mind go anywhere other than you, your board and the water, it's guaranteed that you'll miss the wave or wipe out completely. Surfing is hard but my goodness, never in my life have I felt such pure flow and elation.

After that first session, I could see why Max didn't want to do anything but work and surf (and hang out with me!). Still, I couldn't help but notice just how little of a social life he seemed to have. While I could understand his need for few friends, the part that bothered me most was that he didn't seem to care about introducing me to any of the people he did see regularly. The handful of times he'd had plans to have dinner with his sister Jules or the 'Foster Fam' boys, it was always on a night when I had Asha. On multiple occasions, I suggested getting a babysitter but

Max was adamant that I not waste my money and that I'd meet them eventually. As much as I wanted to believe what Bertie had said about a lack of sex didn't mean Max wasn't romantically into me, I was starting to feel like I'd waded into the Friend Zone.

Although the whole 'rip off each other's clothes' stage of our relationship didn't seem to be in the near future, the 'eventually meeting his friends and family' stage did come sooner than expected when I walked into Max's apartment on a sunny Saturday morning. His brother-in-law Chris was sitting on Max's lounge drinking coffee. The first thing I noticed was that Chris looked a whole lot like Jeremy Clarkson from *Top Gear*. The second thing I noticed was that he had his shoes on Max's coffee table. Wondering where this fell on Max's scale of 'Disrespecting My Cleanliness' (one being a water ring on the table and ten being a floater in the toilet), I figured this fell somewhere around a seven. However, Max didn't seem fussed. In fact, he was happily filling up drink bottles and packing us snacks for our planned walk to Tamarama while I got to hear about Chris's life as a sports coach in Canberra. Apparently, he was just up for the weekend to attend a dinner in Bondi with a bunch of his players. Before I could go too deep, Max was ushering me out the door.

When we got to the footpath, Max detoured from our typical route. 'Let's walk this way – I want to grab my jumper from my car.'

About two minutes later, Max stopped at a Porsche and opened the door. Confused, I asked, 'Is this Chris's car?'

'No, it's mine,' Max replied casually.

So far I'd seen Max drive two 'RRs' and a ute. How had I missed his Porsche? 'Since when?' I asked playfully.

'Since ages … I've owned this one for a few years.'

I responded with a little 'ha' that meant 'well, I'll be damned'. He locked his car and we headed back toward Tamarama.

'Your brother-in-law seems nice,' I said.

'Such a legend.'

'Jules also sounds wonderful. I hope I don't sound needy but I really would like to meet her.'

Max clasped my hand. 'You're not needy. You will meet her, I promise. It's just … I just need to take things slow. I've actually been talking about it with my psych.'

Instantly, I felt like a dickhead for pushing Max. The man was an orphan with an ex-alcoholic fiancé, for fuck's sake. 'Is this the same psych you saw with Bec?'

'Yeah, he's in Glebe.'

'Glebe? Since you guys saw him together, I just assumed he was based in the States.'

'Nah, he's always been based in Oz. We did tele-appointments with him. Although we did see him a few times in the US when he flew over.' Max crossed the road toward Marks Park and I followed.

'Sorry, I'm distracting you from your point. What does he think about wanting to take things slow?'

'He helped me see that I struggle to get close to people as a form of self-preservation. When you lose both your parents in an instant, you become acutely aware of how fragile everything is. As a result, I'm afraid to form attachments.'

'This all makes a lot of sense.'

Max paused when he got to the lookout over Bondi Beach. I walked to his side and we both silently stared at Australia's most iconic beach. The water had never looked bluer. Max started to speak.

'Want to know something? Because of you, I've done more talking than ever during my therapy sessions. Most of the time, I just go in and we silently play chess for an hour. I can tell you're worried about where my head's at ... Trace, I can feel myself being pulled to you. I really feel like we have something special here.'

The smile that appeared on my face could have illuminated the Sydney Cricket Ground. Finally, Max was acknowledging that we were more than friends. He could feel it too. Suddenly, I found the courage to ask, 'Then why haven't you tried to have sex with me yet?'

Max laughed and pulled me in for a hug. 'Because I'm not like other blokes. I adore YOU and want all of that, but I'm not motivated by sex. I'm motivated by this.' Just then, Max kissed my forehead. 'Believe it or not, I'm not one of those guys who wants to get in your pants every minute. It's your beautiful mind and heart that I really want.'

And just like that, all my insecurities disappeared. I nuzzled into his neck.

Max squeezed me tight before adding, 'Plus babe, you know what they say, what starts with a bang, ends in a fizzle.'

CHAPTER 13

A Trivial Pursuit?

The good news: we finally banged. The bad news: it was a total fizzle.

Because I'm fully aware that my mum and daughter will no doubt be reading this book at some point, I'm going to spare the details of the disappointing bedroom life that Max and I had. But for as underwhelming (and infrequent) as the sex was (like, I've never been so underwhelmed in my entire life and I've sat and watched paint dry), I will say that the cuddles were top-notch. Some people 'spoon' but Max 'cocooned' and it was like being back in the womb. Blissful, secure, held by unconditional love, the cocoon was so spectacular that I decided I could live without sizzle.

After all, how can you expect to have it all in your forties? When chatting with a girlfriend about Max, I explained just how different our paths had been. I'd grown up with Snugglepot and Cuddlepie as parents and he'd grown up in and out of foster families. A true loner, he didn't rely on friends and genuinely enjoyed his own company. I, on the other hand, have always gotten a lot of security and energy from having a tight-knit family unit and friend circle. But you know what they say: opposites attract, and sometimes, you just have to accept that relationships are a dance. Ultimately, I asked myself: what do you want more? Someone who ticks every single box and probably doesn't exist, or a solid human who has your back, makes you laugh, pushes you to put yourself first and has a few quirky bits? Sure, I had a question mark or two about 'us' but I certainly wasn't about to throw it all in because of the physical and social issues.

But then something happened at the start of spring that made me wonder if there was a darker side to Max I should be wary of. While at dinner at Fu Manchu in Darlinghurst, Max's phone rang – it was Ana. Max leaned in and touched my forearm. 'Bub, I have to answer this. I also have to warn you that I'm about to go slightly Harvey Specter so brace yourself,' he said, referencing a character from the TV show *Suits*.

And that, he did. Can I just say that trying to disappear into a plate of dumplings is something I never anticipated silently praying for? And yet, Max's tone and demeanour made me want nothing more than to be surrounded by a forcefield of flour. It was hard to piece together the entire story because I could only hear one side, but it sounded like one of the family office's employees wanted her bonus early because she'd taken out bridging finance on her home in Mosman.

Max spat into the phone, 'Poor personal financial decisions do not warrant an early bonus. If anything, they warrant a strike against her name because she's a fucking moron and we don't need fucking morons working with us. I told her not to take out that loan in the first place. She can wait. Don't pay her a cent.'

Max hung up and I did my best to try and act like I wasn't horrified by his behaviour by asking, 'Dumpling?'

'I'm so sorry. I hate when I have to be the bad guy. Yes, give me all the dumplings, Dumpling,' Max replied in a voice that made him seem like a completely rational human who hadn't just been a c-word three seconds earlier.

Over the course of dinner, it was incredible to witness Max change back to being calm, kind and engaging. He became particularly enthusiastic when one of our dishes arrived on a beautiful chopping board and I mentioned that the wood smelled exactly like the camphor laurel trees I used to love in my early childhood. Before I knew it, Max had our waiter telling us all about the artisan who made them, the type of wood he used and how they 'elevate' each dining experience. Much to Max's delight, we learned that we could buy one from the restaurant. And so, when paying our bill, Max proudly bought a camphor-scented chopping board for me. 'I hope you like it.'

I did (and do) like it. But I was still trying to reconcile the two versions of Max I'd been on a date with. Feeling like I needed a bit of alone time, I took a page out of Max's playbook and told him I was exhausted and wanted to sleep in my own bed. He didn't seem to mind that I broke our weekly Wednesday dinner and Bondi sleepover date and happily offered to drive me back to the Northern Beaches. I told him not to be silly because he was only ten minutes from his place and driving me home would be at least an hour round-trip for him.

Max insisted, 'I want to. Plus, it means I get to spend more time with you, which is worth it.'

Even though I still didn't like the 'Harvey Specter Max' I saw in the restaurant, I thought the ride home was a lovely gesture and accepted. This sort of kindness and generosity wasn't something I'd been used to. When we arrived at my apartment, Max planted a kiss on my forehead, leaned back and looked me in the eye with a gentle smile. 'I know you have a big two days at work so let's catch up Saturday. The weather is supposed to be shit, so how about I come around to yours for board games and tea?'

'Board games and tea?' I asked with a cocked head.

'If we can't train our bodies, at least we can train our minds,' Max said half-jokingly.

While trying to drift off to sleep later that night, I thought about the way Max had spoken to Ana. Sure, I'd seen that type of behaviour in the workplace but never in a million years did I think Max had that type of venom inside him. Every time we'd hung out, I'd actually taken note of how warm, calm and even-keeled he was. Was this what 'Investment Banker Max' was like? It made me wonder if there were other versions I didn't know yet.

When Saturday arrived, 'shit' didn't even begin to describe the weather. The sky was falling, the wind was angry and the only positive thing was the sound of raindrops hitting the roof. Arguably the perfect soundtrack for our indoor date around my coffee table, Max and I listened to the rain while trying to play Trivial Pursuit. Key word being 'trying'. Apparently, there's Trivial Pursuit and then there's Trivial Pursuit: Master Edition. As someone who'd pretty much only been playing Operation and Uno for the last decade, I was not prepared for the doozies Max was throwing my way. Much to my surprise, Max didn't seem to know many of the answers either.

'If these were maths questions, I'd get all of them,' Max said off-handedly while getting up to refill our teacups.

I picked up the game's box and pointed to the small print at the bottom. 'It says here, "Reveal your inner genius." Come on, reveal the Mensan!'

Max walked back with our teas and a bag of Snakes. After setting our cups on the coffee table, he started pulling out the Snakes colours he didn't eat. Like 'gooey' things, Max apparently didn't like any gelatinous serpent lollies that were yellow or green. (I'm sure he delivered a man-ologue at some point about why he did this but I must have been too busy eating the discarded Snakes to have taken it in …)

'Hey! Sugar addict – it's your go,' I said nudging his arm.

'I think I'm over the pursuit of the trivial.'

'Me too. Let's do something easier. Let's do the *Good Weekend* quiz!' I hopped up from the floor and grabbed the paper from my kitchen bench. 'I love the quiz!' I said before plopping back down on the floor next to Max. 'Okay, ready?'

Max, mid-chew on an orange snake, nodded.

'From which European language is the word "gastro" derived?'

Max thought for a moment.

'And I'm sorry if it's too soon to hear the word gastro,' I added sympathetically.

Max smiled and answered, 'Greek.'

I checked the answer legend. 'Yes! Alright, what is the formal name of a guitar pick?'

'Not a clue.'

'Me neither. Who would know that?' I checked the answer. 'Plectrum. Now that's a fact that's definitely not going to live rent-free in my head.'

'Give me another.'

'Oh! You'll know this for sure! It's a maths one that you'll no doubt be able to do in your head. What's the inverse square root of 3659 divided by …'

Max interrupted sharply, 'Nope. Not doing it. Nup.'

'Come on, you're the maths guy!'

'My brain is fried from thinking about numbers all week, Bub. Don't make me do maths on a Saturday.'

Before I could push back, Max stood up and moved from the floor to my lounge and opened his book. 'Let me just read about other outliers.'

Max was holding a copy of Malcolm Gladwell's *Outliers*. I'd recently read it and was surprised to hear that Max viewed himself as an outlier. He'd often go on tangents about being a contrarian but an outlier? For the next hour or so, we kept our heads buried in books and magazines, only coming up for air to share interesting thoughts on something we'd read. I'm pretty sure this came out of thin air because I do not recall Malcolm Gladwell spending any time on conspiracy theories in his book, but Max got my attention so he could share one of his many conspiracy theories.

'See that?' Max asked while pointing out my window to a Telstra cable running along the street. 'That's how government officials distract us.'

'From what?'

'From the fact that we're all just living in a simulation and being used as guinea pigs.'

Thinking Max was taking the piss, I fobbed his comment off with a 'pfft'.

'I'm serious, T. The actual leaders of the world are using us to understand disease, climate change and, this goes without saying, amass enormous wealth. It's like *The Matrix*.'

'I've actually never seen *The Matrix*.'

Max looked even more horrified than the one time I saw him accidentally eat a green snake. 'You've never seen *The Matrix*? This is unacceptable.'

'It came out in 1999, right? I remember everyone was raving about it but my life was nothing but Sydney Olympics prep at the time.'

Max was standing at this point and instructing me to do the same. 'T – you're literally the hardest working human I've ever met, and I know that kind of work ethic comes with sacrifices. But not seeing *The Matrix*? Come on. Grab your raincoat. We're going to Video Ezy.'

Even in 2016, walking into a video rental store felt like taking a step back in time; a time when viral mindfulness quotes were 'be kind, rewind' and 'laminated' was still a word people used when talking about membership cards. Unfortunately for Max, he didn't have his Video Ezy card in his wallet and the shop assistant didn't have a 'Max Tavita' in the database.

'Can you look up my account by my address?'

The assistant typed in Max's Bondi address. 'It's not coming up. Sorry.'

Max furrowed his brow and bit his lip. 'Ahh! Try Harvey. Harvey Specter.' Max turned to me while the assistant typed away. 'Fucking hell, Ana! She set this account up for me ages ago and I feel like she was messing with me and made my name Harvey.'

'I'm sorry, sir. I don't have any *Suits* alias accounts in the database either,' the assistant said in a deadpan voice.

Max had a look of defeat on his face. 'Do you have an account?'

'No ... and I really don't feel like signing up for something that's going to be non-existent in the very near future. This divorcée has enough paperwork to do.'

'I really want you to see *The Matrix* though,' Max said like a sad child.

'I promise to add it to my bucket list. But for now, let's get out of 1999, Harvey.'

CHAPTER 14

Things are Heating Up

When my dad died and grief came knocking on my door, I wasn't shocked. Naive to its true depths, but not shocked. After all, we all know that grief is part of the deal when we lose a loved one. However, when my marriage ended and grief showed up, I was well and truly baffled. For starters, the only emotions I'd anticipated feeling were relief, gratitude and hope. Sure, I also expected a bit of frustration and anxiety from time to time but I never could have imagined the intense sadness I'd feel for the loss of the family I *thought* I would get to have. Turns out, divorce grief is a thing.

What's strange about divorce grief is that you're not always mourning the loss of what *was*. In many cases, like my own, you're more likely to be mourning the loss of what *could have been*. Throughout 2015 and 2016, I had to consciously lay to rest the *idea* of the happily ever after I'd dreamed of for Asha and me. No stranger to the brain fog, insomnia and panic attacks that love to hang out with grief, I was much better equipped to reach for tools like journaling, therapy and exercise to work through the process. Still – I underestimated just how mentally fatiguing it would be to continue to work at my usual hectic pace while simultaneously raising Asha, navigating the throes of divorce and trying to build a relationship with Max. I was burnt out and began toying with the idea of taking a leave of absence.

With four to five months off, I could power through life-admin paperwork, take Asha out of before- and after-school care, spend more time with her, catch up on sleep, focus on my health and pay proper attention to what Max and I were evolving into. That last item felt particularly important because I could feel things were getting serious. Even though I had not wanted to introduce Max to Asha until I knew our relationship was going to be long-term, our 76-square-metre apartment made it hard to hide the fact that I had a new 'friend' in my life.

To help ease the process, Asha and Max first met via FaceTime. It was adorable to watch them happily chat through the phone about school, netball and the hierarchy of lollies. While their virtual friendship flourished and we continued to date most Wednesdays and every other weekend, Max and I started speaking (hypothetically) about how we'd work together to form a family unit that aligned with our shared values. Although he was still someone I'd class as a slow burn, I was fully confident that Max was deeply committed to investing in a future with Asha and me.

And so, just when Sydney's foliage was springing back to life, Max and I teed up a time for him to meet Asha at Centennial Park. Just as I'd hoped, the laughter and connection they shared on their FaceTime chats flowed into real life. Asha was six at the time and loved having a fresh set of eyes to watch her do zoomies on her scooter before attempting to climb up the playground fire pole instead of simply sliding down it like the other kids.

'I'll do it my own self!' declared Asha after Max offered to give her a boost.

I smiled, watching Asha make what would have been her fifteenth attempt to climb up the pole. 'She's always been so determined.'

'Wonder where she gets that from,' Max said with a knowing look.

Even though we'd been dating for six months, I was still taken aback by how capable, smart and beautiful Max always managed to make me feel ... even when I was at a playground holding wet wipes, a half-eaten apple and a takeaway coffee I'd yet to take a sip of.

'Max! Max! Mum! Max!' Asha yelled. 'I did it!'

Like any good hype squad would, we erupted in cheers and applause.

'That's amaaaaazzziiiing! Unreal, Jerry!' Max said in a very excited tone.

'Jerry!?' Asha asked with her arms akimbo and head cocked to the side.

'Ya look like a Jerry to me, kid!'

While proudly running down the ramp to us, Asha laughed hysterically at her new nickname. *Max's love language is nicknames. Cute.*

'Alright, Jerry. Are you ready for that chocolate milkshake we promised you?' I asked.

Asha, now wide-eyed and sporting a huge smile, nodded her head. When I went to grab her scooter and helmet, Max immediately offered to carry it, a gesture that did not go unnoticed.

Another thing that didn't go unnoticed was how engaged he was with Asha. Not only did Max sound genuinely interested in all of Asha's stories, thoughts and opinions about anything and everything, he was also able to match her energy. Energy that could be described as a twelve-week-old puppy with a new toy meets Cher's career in 1989. Impressive, to say the least.

While Asha was slurping down her milkshake, Max and I spoke about my upcoming trip to the US for eBay's Luminary Awards. My team and I were being honoured for the virtual reality department store shopping experience we'd created with Myer. I was ecstatic because on top of an expenses-paid work trip to California and each team member receiving a $10,000 reward, I was getting the opportunity to demo the headsets and experience to eBay's US executive team. Max, who (surprisingly) didn't have any stories or humble brags to share about Silicon Valley or venture capitalists, was thrilled for me.

'How many "Make America Great Again" hats do you think you'll see?' he asked sarcastically.

Seeing as this trip was happening in the lead-up to the infamous US presidential election that nearly broke the internet, it was hard to enter a room where you didn't hear the words 'Trump' or 'Hillary' bouncing off the walls, even in Australia. In a way, it was like a car crash that nobody could look away from, including me. While I was interested in the candidates and psyche of US voters, Max was completely enthralled by what impact it would have on the global economy.

'I doubt I'll see many in San Jose … I get the impression that Silicon Valley is with her.'

'From what my friends in New York are saying, I get the impression that the rest of the country is with him. I think he's going to get in. And I also think the stock market is going to boom.'

Before I had the chance to respond, Asha, who'd just licked the remaining chocolate from the walls of her cup, was bouncing our way. 'Can we do another lap? I want to do another lap!'

Max smiled. 'I've got another lap in me if you do.'

I looked at Asha, who was already putting her helmet on her head. 'One more. And then we've got to get home.'

Instantly, a smile beamed across Asha's face. Within seconds, we heard the click of her chin strap and she was off!

'I think she likes you.'

Max, who gave me a playfully smug look, nodded in agreement. 'Who wouldn't?'

'Give yourself an uppercut, Sunshine.'

•

For as many pinch-me moments that I had in the US with my eBay colleagues, part of me couldn't wait to get home to see Max and Asha again. That little taster of what weekends could be like as a 'unit' felt wholesome, calm and exactly like the type of dynamic I was looking for. While most of my days were scheduled from sunrise to sunset with presentations, meetings, demos, meals and activities, I still managed to find time to send Max loads of pics and hop on FaceTime for chats here and there. One of the best calls happened while I was getting ready for a team dinner on my final day. Knowing it was midday in Australia, I called Max, expecting to find him at work in the city or having lunch. When he answered, I found him driving through a familiar-looking neighbourhood.

'Are you in Freshwater?' I asked while leaning my phone against the bathroom mirror so I could tie my hair up in my go-to mum bun.

'Sure am. The weather is too nice to be at work. Thought I'd go for a drive and look at a house I've been thinking about putting an offer on.'

'What are you doing looking at properties in my neck of the woods?' I asked coyly.

'I love your little unit but I want you and Asha to be more comfortable, especially if I'm going to be spending more time around.'

Between the reflection of my face in the mirror and reverse camera, I knew there was no hiding my excitement for the idea of Max moving to Freshwater. 'I support this thinking! What did you find?'

'Four bedder on Evans Street.'

While I was making sure my jaw wasn't visibly on the floor at the thought of him buying a *four-bedroom* home on one of Freshwater's most sought-after streets, Max added, 'I'm just concerned it's that little bit too far from the city. I really need to be able to get into work within fifteen minutes. I would retire, but the longer I work, the sooner we can buy a big fuck-off house.' My excitement dialled down a notch when he said that. *But I don't need a big fuck-off house.*

Unsure what financial emergency couldn't be solved via VPN and broadband, I tried to pretend like that made sense. I also tried to not get my hopes up that we'd be playing house anytime soon. Therapist Bertie's words played in my head. 'Focus on building the relationship slowly.' That evening in the hotel, I turned to my journal.

It feels like a lot has changed in the last month. I have comfort in the fact you have said you're not dating anyone else, you want to be with me and you're making a lot of effort to spend time together when it's possible for me.

I feel safe and secure and like you have my best interests at heart. It's as though I have someone I can trust. I know it's still early days in the grand scheme of things but I also know you're a solid human being and I like that.

I love the time we spend together and I am enjoying getting to know you better. Slowly and surely. I love that we talk every day. I love that you're always checking in on me and I love that you don't put any pressure on me to spend more time with you when I can't. You're patient with me and I love that.

And you've met Asha. That's big for me. And you're great with her. I look forward to more times together, especially in summer.

I'm glad you're not flashy with your money and things. That would be a big turn-off for me. You are kind and generous but not arrogant or flashy. I like that.

Above everything, you make me feel good. You make me feel interesting and smart. You make me laugh. I enjoy every moment I spend with you and I never want it to finish. Just more time together that's what I'd like and the rest will take care of itself. Xx

CHAPTER 15

Privy to Information

In early September, Max called while I was walking home from the gym. I had my water bottle, towel and jumper in my hands, which caused me to perform quite an impressive juggling act before answering. Max, who'd apparently just finished a run, sounded more excited than usual.

'I don't want to talk too much about it over the phone but I'm privy to some information regarding something that's happening in the States. Do you think we could find some time to talk about it in person over the next few weeks? It's time-sensitive.'

'Trump's winning, isn't he? Are you throwing money into a pool?' I said half-jokingly.

Max playfully defended himself, 'No, I would never stoop from chief investment officer to political punter.'

'Didn't think so. Sure, how about you come to mine Wednesday evening?'

'Done.'

When Max arrived at my place a few days later, he was still in his suit which made me think he must have come straight from work instead of going home to change. *Bet he didn't pack an overnight bag.* In an effort to hide my disappointment that he didn't intend on staying, I poured two glasses of wine and started cooking dinner.

'I have a little gift for you,' Max said while slipping his hand inside his jacket. He pulled out a small packet of what appeared to be some sort of seasoning. 'I saw this Kashmiri red chilli powder and thought of you.'

It was such a thoughtful gift. Max must have remembered the story I'd recently told him about eating my way through India after Dad died. I took the packet from Max and looked at the label. 'This looks incredible. Thank you.' When I flipped it over, I saw he'd left the price tag on. *Eighteen bucks for 100 grams? Yeesh!* 'Do you mind if I spice up the chicken I had planned for tonight?'

'Spice away!'

As I began to prep chicken breast, potatoes and Greek salad ingredients, Max took a seat at the bench and lowered his voice. 'I don't like mixing business with my personal life but Jules mentioned that I should probably have a chat to you about it.'

Baffled, I gave Max a look that said, 'Do tell …'

'Remember how I mentioned that something's about to happen in the US? Well, I can't say too much but it's going to mean some movement in the markets which I'm going to take advantage of for my family office clients and myself. Jules and Chris want to invest too … that's when you came up. Jules thought maybe I can help you too.'

Even though I'd worked for a start-up hedge fund in my early twenties, taken a few mandatory financial ethics courses and held shares in eBay, I admit that mergers and markets talk wasn't a language I readily understood. I decided to proceed with caution. 'Tell me a bit more. Is this a long- or short-term investment?'

Max took a sip of his wine. 'Short. You'll have your money back after the election. But technically, nobody is supposed to know about it until then.'

As Max's words 'nobody is supposed to know about it until then' rolled in my head, my mind flashed to Roxy Jacenko, whose husband, Oliver Curtis, had just been jailed for insider trading.

'Isn't this considered insider trading?'

'I know it sounds like it, but I've spoken to our barrister. According to Schedule 28 and Law 5.13 it's above board ... Look, it's totally up to you. Normally, I don't mix work with my personal life, but Jules suggested I offer it to you and I want to help you out. I know how stressed you've been about everything. This is a step you can take to become financially independent. It could even give you the cushion you need to finally take that sabbatical you've been talking about.'

I took a moment to think while placing the potatoes into the oven. 'What's the expected return?'

Max, who was now up and helping make the salad, shook his head as if he could hardly believe it himself. 'You could double your money. And at the very least, you'll get your initial investment back in full.'

'Is there a minimum amount I'd need to put in?'

'Whatever you can afford. Don't leave yourself short.'

'Okay, I'll think about it.'

Max drizzled dressing on the salad before walking it to the table. 'Bub, I know you love being independent and want to take care of things. I respect that and it's one of the things I love most about you. But this is a small way I can help ease the load for you. I want you to be financially independent and if I can help, I'd like to be a part of that.'

If I'd been in a relationship with an electrician and he wanted to invest my money, it would have been a hard no. But Max wasn't an electrician; he was a highly knowledgeable, intelligent and dedicated investment executive who I'd listened to and watched work through the night for his clients. On top of trusting him with making me money, I admit that I kind of *needed* more money. At the time, I had mounting legal fees for my divorce and astronomical childcare costs. Even though I was keeping up with everything – just – the thought of having a buffer of funds while I took some much-needed time off to look after myself and health was very seductive.

Of course, Max knew all of this.

That weekend, my girlfriend from uni, Kelly, came down from the Gold Coast to stay with me. Even though we wanted maximum girl time, Kelly was dying to meet The Slow Burn she'd been hearing so much about. Hoping to do dinner with Max, I called The Apollo, one of our favourite places to eat in Potts Point, to make a reservation but they were completely booked out. When I relayed the news to Max and suggested we try The Butler, he was adamant that he or Ana could pull some strings and get us in. A few minutes later, it was confirmed – we had a table for three booked at 7 pm. I didn't know why Max and Ana had pull at The Apollo but I was grateful nonetheless.

While some people get nervous about introducing a prospective partner to their parents, I get nervous about introducing them to my friends. On some level, I want their approval but mostly I just want my partner and girlfriends to love each other every bit as much as I love them.

Kelly and I grabbed a pre-dinner drink at The Butler while Max finished up work.

'Tell me how things are going with The Slow Burn,' she said as soon as we sat down.

'You'll be happy to hear that things are actually heating up! We've been spending a lot more time together and he met Asha. They get along so well, which makes me so happy. I cannot tell you how refreshing it is to date someone who likes the same pace of life as me. I also feel like he's bringing out a side of me that I haven't seen for a long time. He's very empowering.'

Kelly was visibly pleased to hear about my happiness. 'In what way?'

In a million ways. 'It doesn't matter if we're talking about work or running or parenting, he always manages to build me up and make me believe that I can accomplish anything. My career is going from strength to strength and he's helping me with some investments. I feel like the future is looking positive for me.'

'And he really has five cars?' Kel quipped with raised eyebrows.

In an effort to not sound offended or lean into any of my own insecurities about the situation, I casually replied, 'He does. We've been together since April and since then, I've been to his apartment and seen four of his five cars in person. The fifth, the Aston Martin, was sold for a profit shortly after he bought it.' I reached for my phone and pulled up the photo he'd sent of it in his garage. 'Look, he put one of those luggage pods on top for his skis.'

Under the photo he'd texted:

Max: Who says supercars are impractical?!!!! The snow has called ... x

Kelly laughed. 'Okay, I believe you.'

I placed my phone on the bar and picked up my glass of wine.

'I'm happy for you, Trace. You deserve to be loved and adored.'

Just as I was feeling a hint of smugness, I got a text from Max.

Max: Sorry, Bub. Not going to make it to dinner. Markets and work are a mess.

For how disappointed I was, I couldn't say I was surprised. Whenever our plans involved meeting someone else, Max often had a last-minute excuse of why he couldn't make it. Perhaps it really was the markets or perhaps he couldn't overcome his social anxiety. I gave him a sympathetic reply before telling Kelly it would be just us.

'You'll meet him some other time,' I said breezily before getting the bill. While we had a fabulous dinner at The Apollo, internally I remained annoyed with Max.

The next morning, Kelly and I were nursing our heads over two very strong cups of tea when Max knocked on the door with newspapers and an apology. Whatever ill-feelings I had about him bailing on us the night before were completely gone when I quickly realised that Kelly and Max had no shortage of things to bond over. For a good part of the morning, Kelly and Max chatted about her career as a high school teacher and current pursuit of a master's degree in maths. Just when they were both sounding way too intelligent for their own good, the conversation shifted to our shared passions of running, surfing and travel. *Things are going well!*

The next morning, I drove Kel to the airport so she could catch her flight home. On the way there, I was thinking about how great our weekend had been and how grateful I was that we got to make up for so much lost ground. I was under the impression that Kel and Max had connected, which gave me a lot of comfort. That is until Kel made a comment that took me a little by surprise.

'You know that investment you were talking about ... I'm sure it's all fine and legit, but just playing devil's advocate for a second – are you sure it's a good idea? I mean, you haven't known Max for *that* long?'

I pondered over her words and reassured her (and myself) that Max was the real deal. I had no reason not to believe him and what he said. After all, he always had my best interests at heart.

A few nights later, I was on the phone with Max, thinking about how happy I was that he'd met at least one of my besties, when he said something that irked me. I was detailing, yet again, the many ways I was exhausted, broken and burnt out after another huge week of work. In fairness, Max could have been trying to put a stop to the broken record I'd become but, at the time, it felt weird when he said, 'Trace – you need a holiday. You haven't had a holiday in ages. I will buy you a first-class ticket to anywhere you want to go.'

Immediately, I told him that while that was an incredibly generous offer, it really wasn't necessary.

'You give and give and give. Who's looking after you, Bub?'

He had a point. And to be honest, it seemed like an authentic gesture of care. However, the enormity and grandiosity of it didn't sit well. I would have felt uncomfortable accepting it for a number of reasons. I thanked him but said I didn't think giving an airline $25,000 would solve any of my problems. Don't get me wrong – at this point in time, I'd never felt more like I was struggling to keep my head above water. The virtual reality project I'd been working on was on top of my existing role of managing a marketing team of sixteen, a task that already had me working from sunrise to sunset. Added to that was full-time single parenting and the enormous amount of admin that comes with dividing assets and making a parenting plan, so it made sense that I was feeling stretched thin. With that being said, I still felt wildly grateful for my job. From the time I was crumbing sausages in high school, I had always valued hard work and independence. If I hadn't had my career, I probably wouldn't have been able to leave my marriage.

'Even though you've been hearing me complain a lot lately, I actually really do love my job,' I said. 'I think I'm just tired.'

Max understood and said he was only looking for ways to help me get back on my feet, which is why I wasn't surprised when, a few weeks later, he brought up the US investment over dinner.

'Have you thought about the opportunity, TT? Do you want me to put a trade through for you?'

Wishing I was someone who felt more confident about investing, I scrunched my nose in apprehension. 'I really can't afford to lose any money. Are you sure there isn't a downside?'

'There's only an upside. At the worst, you'll get your money back. Basically, this is just an opportunity to double your money.'

'Okay. What's involved logistically? Do I need to create an account?'

'I'll put it through with the money that Jules, Chris and I are putting in. It'll be your money though.'

I took a deep breath and decided I wanted to do it. 'Alright, I'm going to transfer some money to you. I don't have a lot.'

'That's fine,' Max said. After taking a bite of food, he added, 'Don't leave yourself short.'

'I've cashed in some of my eBay and PayPal shares recently, so I'll use that.'

The next day, Max sent me the bank details to make the transfer.

Tracy: Are you sure it's worth doing $10k?
Max: LOL of course, Babe. Just throw in what you're comfortable with.
Max: Get the fire going.

On 4 October 2016, I transferred $10,000 to an account named GSC8.

Above: True 80s kids, my brothers and I were excited to help Dad unpack our first computer, a Commodore 64.

Right: Me in my Stadium Australia days in the lead-up to the 2000 Olympics in Sydney.

Left: Dad and I making sure we got our daily dose of Vitamin C(heese).

Above: Celebrating Mum and Dad's thirtieth wedding anniversary in Lennox Head in March 2002. None of us could ever have imagined he'd be gone just five months later.

Left: Snugglepot and Cuddlepie making friends in Binna Burra (Gold Coast Hinterland) during a picnic day in 2002.

Right: Teaching the best kids in the world! India, 2002

Right: Three generations of stripe lovers. Mum (aka Nanny Bootcamp), Asha and I took a girls trip to Point Danger in December 2016.

Below: Our first holiday – 'Max' bringing beach bike vibes before we took our last selfie of 2016 when elebrating NYE at Halcyon House in Cabarita.

Left: 'Max' and I taking a super serious selfie while waiting for our kombucha cocktails.

Right: Classic Saturday morning of 'Max' catching some Zs at my place after a hard night 'working the markets'.

Above: 'Max' and I having dinner at the Beach Cafe in Byron Bay in January 2017.

Right: Our final beach walk during our July 2017 trip to Byron Bay. Two days later, he'd be in handcuffs.

Still frame from the footage I watched of Hamish being arrested in front of his Bondi apartment on 11 July 2017. *Courtesy of NSW Police*

Leaving court with Detective Senior Constable Tom Zadravec on 14 June 2019. Had to learn how to swim through the sea of reporters covering the case. *Adam Yip Photography/Newspix*

From left to right: Bec Rosen and her sons, Karen Lowe, me, Lorraine and Peter Cross, and Glenn Pickard gathering in June 2019 after the court hearing. *Adam Yip Photography/Newspix*

The Australian journalist and *Who the Hell is Hamish?* podcast creator Greg Bearup and I sharing the story with Sky News in August 2019.

Below: 2023 – Soaking up the morning rays with Asha.

Above: Friend, supersleuth and protector Cath Coleman catching a film with me at the Westpac OpenAir cinema.

CHAPTER 16

Forty-one Candles

By the time I turned forty-one that November, I had bitten the bullet and gotten my sabbatical approved. And just like that, I had a few months to rest, recharge and rediscover what I really wanted from life. The plan? I wanted to go 'inward' through yoga, my journal, trips away and the stack of to-be-read books that had been towering next to my bed for far too long. My ultimate goal was to figure out how I could earn the money needed to keep Asha and myself in the Sydney lifestyle we were accustomed to without sacrificing my mental or physical health.

Max showed me just how on board he was with my 'sustainable yet still abundant' career goals on my birthday. Although I'd continuously said I didn't need anything from him but love and support, Max showed up on my doorstep with a sleek new yoga mat, activewear from Nimble (a brand I'd long admired from shop windows), the latest Nike running shoes, a pair of stunning sunglasses, a short-sleeve wetsuit and a duffle bag to cart it all around. For how grateful I was for such a thoughtful and generous gift, I did feel slightly embarrassed at the thought of how much it must have cost. Max may have been used to spending huge amounts of money on gifts, but I certainly wasn't.

When I wasn't in tree pose or mapping out my ideal day, I spent most of my newfound downtime tidying up my life admin to-do list and learning what it felt like to sleep for a full seven hours. I also found time to book a nine-day trip over Christmas to stay with Max at Halcyon House in Cabarita Beach. Since Asha was going to be with her dad, this seemed like the perfect opportunity for Max and me to spend a longer stretch of time together. Even better, he was going to get to meet Mum and my brothers since we were heading up their way.

Despite the money still coming in from my annual leave, there was something nerve-racking about being off from work for such an extended period of time. Conscious of how expensive this trip could be, I told Max I would be just as happy in a beach shack or camping in the sand dunes ... just as long as we could surf all day and eat well at night. Max, who didn't blink twice at the $800–1000 per night room rate on Halcyon House's website, argued that we should splurge because it was our first Christmas and New Year together. He also pointed out that it's expensive everywhere that time of year before saying, 'Fuck it, let's do it! I'll cover it.'

As someone who was not used to dropping that kind of money, let alone a boyfriend dropping that kind of money, I couldn't help but look for ways to help cover the costs, which is how I found myself helping Max sell a few items on eBay. For as long as we'd been dating, he'd had a $10,000 race bike leaning against his living room wall that I'd never seen him ride. He also had quite an impressive selection of never-worn luxury sunglasses that would have been collecting dust if Max's apartment had any.

One evening when we'd been chatting about why he only owned two wine glasses – Riedel, of course – Max mentioned he wanted to donate it all because he wanted to go 'full minimalist'. I'd heard Max speak about not wanting to attract the type of people who were only interested in being friends due to his wealth before but during this particular chat, he explained that he also felt like he just didn't want or need anything more than his surfboard, running shoes and picnic blanket for us to catch a moonrise. As much as I could relate to not needing much 'stuff', the savvy saver in me couldn't bear the idea of Max just giving the bike and sunnies away so I offered to list the lot.

'How about I give you fifty per cent of whatever the items sell for?' he said. 'That will make me feel better about you using your time away from eBay selling things on eBay.'

I laughed and raised my eyebrows in approval. 'Why don't we put it toward our holiday? Halcyon House is not cheap.'

The bike went for $6000 while the collection of never-worn sunnies, shoes and a high-end coffee grinder collected close to $2000. When Max handed me a stack of $100 notes a few weeks later, it reminded me of something that had happened quite early in our relationship.

Probably a few months in, Max walked into my apartment and placed a stack of $100 notes on my kitchen bench. Taking note of how much green there was and guesstimating that the stack was a solid 12 centimetres high, I immediately thought, 'Is this guy a drug dealer?' When I sternly asked Max why an obscenely large wad of cash was sitting on my bench, he said he was lending some money to a friend. *Sure.* Worried it was obtained illegally and also slightly worried that Max thought I was the type of girl who'd be impressed with a stack of dollar-dollar-bills-yo, I told him that I never wanted to see that type of cash in my apartment again. Max instantly apologised and reiterated that he was just helping out a friend in a tight spot. He said he'd gotten the money out of the bank that day and didn't want to leave it in his car. My gut suspected something else but just didn't know what …

As soon as I got the opportunity, I deposited my portion of the bike and sunnies money into my account with visions of me using it to surprise Max with nice meals and adventures up the coast. Just a few days later, my money concerns were tempered yet again when Max called while I was driving into the city for a work Christmas party. (Sabbatical or not, you don't miss the work Christmas party!) After chatting about how I planned on getting home and if I was going to be in good enough form for our running date the following day, Max excitedly shared, 'Oh, by the way, that little investment you made has given you a one hundred per cent return.'

'What do you mean?' I asked, thinking he was telling me that I was simply getting 100 per cent of my money back.

'It means you've doubled your money.'

'Really? Wow. Why didn't I start investing in the stock market sooner?' I asked half-jokingly.

Max took this rhetorical question as an opportunity to talk about my work. 'I've been thinking about your career. Not just the part where it prevented you from watching the cinematic masterpiece that is *The Matrix* but about how much you put in and how little you're getting out. It kills me that someone with your calibre of skills and endurance to withstand sixteen-hour days doesn't have financial freedom yet. So much of me just wants to take away your need to work so you can focus on you.'

I could tell Max was coming from a place of love but the idea of him 'saving' me from my 'need to work' wasn't sitting that well. I wasn't sure how to respond but before I had a chance to say anything, Max asked, 'Who's your super with?'

'MLC.'

'What's your balance?'

'Not sure. I'll have a look and let you know.'

'Have a look at what the fees are. Would also be good to know what the mix of funds is … There's a reason high-net-worth families have specialised investment people like me working for them. The sheep go with the big superfunds but they're honestly just run by thieves who aren't working hard enough. Most people could be making more money from their hard work, but they just don't know it. Or know how.'

Again, I told him I'd look into it. I was a bit taken aback by his keen and somewhat mood-killing interest in my finances, but I had a Christmas party to get to. My team was getting together at Barangaroo for dinner and drinks and I had tapas and margies in my eyes.

A few weeks later, I asked Max for his email so I could send him my superfund statement.

Max: maxtavita75@gmail.com

Tracy: Why 75? Isn't your birthday 1974?

Max: It wasn't available. x

The next Saturday morning, Max turned up at mine as planned. He was enraged about my super. 'They're thieves! They're just thieves, T. Look at the fees ... that's where your money is going. You should see what some of my clients are earning off their money.'

I shrugged, preoccupied with my breakfast. 'I'm sure they're working with much bigger balances, though.'

'You know I want you to be financially secure and independent,' Max said. 'Honestly, I feel like I could do much better with your money than what those thieves are doing.'

'Really?'

'Have you ever considered setting up a self-managed superfund?'

'Definitely not. I have never invested in anything other than high performance activewear,' I joked.

'Look, self-managed superfunds aren't for everyone and I've seen them fail many times. Mostly because it's some tradie thinking he can buy a holiday home or invest in crypto with it. But I'd be happy to manage it for you.'

I finished the toast I was eating. 'That's a really kind offer, but I'll have to think about this. I'm not very adventurous with my finances.'

'Of course. Look, I manage a fund for Jules if you ever want to talk to her about it.'

'What are the fees?'

'A minimum of ten minutes in the cocoon position every night,' Max said with a wink.

I smiled and said, 'I'll think about it.'

When Max first mentioned managing my superannuation, my mind did not immediately flash to news headlines of women losing everything to Nigerian email phishing scams. In no way did I think that the man who held me at night was trying to destroy my life. I had listened to, discussed and overheard countless conversations about his investments and trades, read reports and seen paperwork and even met co-workers. From everything I'd heard and seen, I thought this totally decent, understated and deeply caring man wanted to look out for me.

In the early weeks of December, Max and I spoke more about the returns he could get me if I established a self-managed superfund that he could manage on my behalf. I asked him many questions about how it would work, what it all meant and the process that would be needed. I googled 'SMSF' and read up on what was required.

We went over the money I would save on fees, as well as the strategy he used with his family office clients and Jules. Convinced that Max was not only completely qualified for the job and confident that he was looking out for my best interests, I gave him the go-ahead. Within days, Max had stacks of pre-filled documents marked with tabs where I needed to sign.

'I want you to go through this carefully and fully understand everything. Anything you aren't sure about, I'm happy to explain to you. This is your future, T. You are in the driver's seat now.'

The first document gave me reason to pause. 'Certificate of Registration of a Company?' I asked.

Max, who was standing next to me while I shuffled through the paperwork at my kitchen bench, explained that it's legally safer to have a corporate trustee manage a fund versus an individual, hence why he'd met with a solicitor and established a company in my name. Evidently, he'd chosen 'T Hall Investments Pty Ltd'.

Next, Max instructed me to transfer the balance from my MLC superfund to a cash fund in preparation for it to be transferred to a yet-to-be-established Westpac business account that I would use to self-manage it. Aside from needing to take a few of those documents to open said business account in the new year, all I had to do was sign on the dotted line ... multiple times. Which I did.

CHAPTER 17

A Christmas Miracle

On Christmas Eve, I kissed Asha goodbye and headed to Max's apartment so we could leave for Cabarita Beach bright and early. Max had recently traded in his VW Amarok for a new Mazda BT50. He got busy packing the car while I curated our road trip playlist and prepped picnic supplies for our planned stop at Woolgoolga. Even though I'd had more free time in my diary, Max and I actually hadn't spent much time together due to work drama at the family office. Evidently, Ana had resigned from her CEO position and the company didn't want to pay her bonus. Max ended up cancelling a date we'd planned in order to meet Ana at Icebergs in Bondi to sort it all out. Because Ana's departure necessitated the urgent recruitment of a new CEO and handover, Max, who was now the acting CEO, was under the pump all day and night.

Eager to get on the road and into 'Tracy and Max' mode as soon as possible, we exchanged Christmas gifts that night. Max had been so generous on my birthday that I didn't know how my selection of books and a t-shirt was going to compare. I knew he'd like the shirt because he told me the exact one he'd had his eye on at Orlebar Brown in Bondi. The real question was – would he be into *Blink* and *Freakanomics*? Turns out, yes, Max was into my non-fiction literary selections. And apparently, I'm into black leather goods. Just like he'd done with my birthday, Max had gone way over the top in the gifting department and bought me Alexander Wang boots, an Acne Studios leather jacket, as well as a raft of cute clothes that he thought would come in handy for our week together at Halcyon House. His gift was way too generous – the boots were $600 and the leather jacket was $2450. But impressively, Max's taste and choices were totally on point and there wasn't one thing I wanted to resize or return.

For how beautiful the gifts were and how much I genuinely appreciated them, I was truly the happiest when Max and I got in the car the next morning and settled in for the nine-hour drive up the coast. With work and the rest of the world in our rear-view mirror, all I could see was our future nine days of beachside picnics, early morning surf sessions and family catch-ups. We pulled into Cabarita Beach just after 4 pm. After checking into our room and showering, Max and I went to dinner at the hotel's restaurant, Paper Daisy. The minute we walked in, I saw a girlfriend from Sydney who was up visiting her family for Christmas. In the flurry of our excitement at bumping into each other, I introduced my friend to Max, who visibly hung back and stayed quiet. *Why is he only social when he wants to be?*

Thankfully, Max was much more cheerful and engaged when we met up with Mum and her friend and then with my older brother, his wife and my nephews. On both occasions, Max earned his unofficial 'Hall pass' to our family when he proved he could talk about sport for hours at a time and agreed that it's sacrilegious to go to a regional town in Australia and not eat at the obligatory Chinese restaurant they all seem to have. When Max ducked out to the loo or was out of earshot, my family leaned in to tell me how much they liked him. This made me happy.

What didn't make me happy was the lack of physical intimacy and the daily trips Max made to the ANZ bank in Byron Bay. Although he cited his need to sign off on trades because Ana wasn't there, I didn't hide the fact I wasn't thrilled that Max hadn't truly 'signed off' for our holiday. A couple of times, Max suggested I go along and grab snacks at the supermarket for the beach or pop into the boutiques while he was in the bank. Other times, I stayed at the hotel and hung by the pool because, as Max would say, 'Brown fat looks better than white fat.' (On the Goldie we say, 'If you can't tone it, tan it!') As much as I didn't want to think negatively, I couldn't help but wonder what could possibly be so urgent in the investment world that Max had to drive an hour round-trip to Byron every day between Christmas and New Year. When I grew tired of my thoughts of some high-net-worth family needing funds for a superyacht purchase, my mind would switch to thinking about my disappointment that we were seven days into our trip and had only had sex once. *Why isn't he all over me? This is prime lovemaking time!*

Like always, Max managed to reassure me that the lack of physical intimacy wasn't something to be concerned about. He wasn't 'like that' but that didn't mean he wasn't attracted to me. To be fair, the way Max clutched my hand and made me laugh felt every bit as satisfying as sex. (Okay, not *every bit* but pretty close.) So did the way he comforted me when he remembered that New Year's Eve was Dad's birthday. While sipping cocktails that had been specifically made with Ketel One vodka as opposed to the vodka that was included in the food and beverages package we'd paid for (because that's what Max drinks), we spoke about Dad and how sad I was that he didn't get to meet and know Asha. Max had a huge smile on his face as he talked about how much Dad would have adored watching her sing, dance and do zoomies on her scooter. Throughout most of our relationship, I had been hesitant to bring up the plane crash that killed Max's parents. But in this moment, it felt right to ask how he felt about them missing out on seeing who he became.

'I was so young when they died that I can't really picture what I'd want from them as an adult, you know? Of course I've wanted them around for all the life milestone moments, but it's hard for me to remember their personalities. My main struggle is the image I have of them dying.'

Shocked by his last statement, I asked, 'You were in the plane?'

'They were in the front. I was in the back.'

When Max told me his parents had died in a plane crash during our first call, it never occurred to me that he could have been in the plane. Apparently, they'd gone down shortly after take-off. He said it all happened so fast and all he remembers was waking up to arms pulling him out of the plane and the image of his parents slumped over in their seats. I had lots of questions but really just wanted to listen.

Eventually, Max redirected the conversation to the fact that we were getting to start a new year together. Because Max and I were in our forties, there was zero expectation that we'd actually make it until midnight. And so, around 10 pm, we walked back to our room and went to bed. While holding me tightly in our little cocoon, Max and I whispered all the things we wanted to do together one day.

Me: 'Trek through Bhutan.'

Max: 'Go on a surf trip to Indo.'

Me: 'Confidently surf a wave bigger than two feet.'

Max: 'Spend a summer with you in Italy.'

Me: 'Run a marathon.'

Max: 'Watch *The Matrix* together.'

Me: 'No, not that.'

Max: 'Spend Australia Day long weekend in Byron Bay.'

Me: 'Yes!'

Aside from the daily trips he'd been making to Byron from Cabarita, Max had previously only been there once or twice because he'd lived overseas for so long. As someone who once considered naming their unborn child 'Byron', I knew I was just the woman to show him around. Even though Max was close to nodding off, I started recounting my childhood memories of chasing whales and dolphins on the bay in a surf catamaran. I couldn't wait to make new memories with Max ... this time surfing Wategos and Tallows. Anxious to get it in the diary, I reached for my phone that was on the bedside table and blocked out Australia Day before looking for more opportunities for us to head that way.

When my eyes landed on 28 March, I asked, 'What are your plans for your birthday?'

'Heading to Byron Bay with you,' Max replied with a cheeky grin.

'I love that plan.'

By the sound of his breathing, I could tell that Max was down for the count. I wasn't too far behind, but as I went to put my phone on the bedside table, I found myself hesitating. Instead, I sat up slightly, opened Google and typed in: 'Max Tavita family plane crash survivor'. *Nothing.*

Max and I spent New Year's Day at the beach and checked out of the hotel the following day. We agreed we could have stayed there forever but parenting duties beckoned. Even though I'd booked the room with my credit card and said Max could transfer me money later, he was adamant about settling the bill himself. Thinking he'd put down a credit card, I was surprised when he pulled out not one but two envelopes of cash and counted out $7900 ('keep the change') for the receptionist. *Why is there always so much cash? And why does this feel as icky as the stack of cash he put on my kitchen bench that day? Is this just something rich people do?*

To be honest, I didn't dwell on it much. Happy and love drunk, I wanted to enjoy the last few hours of 'Tracy and Max' time before returning to reality. Although, I will say that reality did feel like an exciting destination. When I got home, I had every intention of grabbing life by the horns. There was a self-managed superfund to set up and a newfound independence to claim. And even though there were lots of things I wanted to say to Max, I saved them for my journal.

What a difference a few months makes. And what an incredible nine days we spent together over Christmas. So easy, so us. Things feel different since we got back. So much more relaxed and comfortable like I just know we are going to be together so I don't have to worry about anything.

And I know you have my back ... I've never felt that before. I miss having my little partner in crime beside me every day. I miss being able to bounce things off you. Anyway, I always have your heart in my thoughts to protect and love. xx

CHAPTER 18

T Hall Investments Pty Ltd

Trying to find a parking spot on Military Road in Mosman is like trying to find a decent coffee in the US. Nearly impossible. (Sorry if you're someone who thinks percolated dishwater is acceptable.) I don't know what stars had to align on that day, 4 January 2016, but by some miracle I whipped my little Golf into a spot just two blocks away from a Westpac bank. On the way there, Cath called, which allowed me to give her a long overdue life update. I described my time away over Christmas and New Year with Max, our plans to head back to Byron for Australia Day and my decision to set up a self-managed superfund – hence my trip to the bank.

I could tell by her tone that Cath wasn't as enthused as I was by that last piece of information. In fact, she was the definition of dubious as she peppered me with questions about why I thought a self-managed fund would do better than my existing retail fund. She wasn't hostile or anything, but I could tell she was silently thinking, *Why rock the boat when you're already sailing smoothly?* However, when I explained that Max was going to manage it for me, I immediately sensed her attitude shift to, *Why the fuck do you trust this guy so much?*

'Are you sure that's a good idea?' she asked. The thing was, Cath hadn't met Max and didn't know anything about his long career in finance. She wasn't there like I was, listening to his conversations, seeing his reports and watching him work. Knowing I didn't have the time to make my case, I politely ended the call, went into Westpac and opened a bank account for T Hall Investments Pty Ltd.

Max and I jetted up to Byron for Australia Day, which we spent sipping gin kombuchas and sunning ourselves at The Pass. I was still in holiday mode afterward and didn't have the energy to tackle the plethora of superfund paperwork Max had given me. By early February, I had yet to have my self-managed superfund up and running. For as enthusiastic as Max was about helping me with the admin side of things, taking this big of a financial step was daunting.

Max, always great at sensing my true feelings, offered some reassurance. 'If at any point you want to take your money out, we can put it back into your Westpac account.'

'You're sure?'

Max replied, 'Absolutely.'

'Okay, so what do I need to do now?' I asked while grabbing a notebook and pen.

Max went on to explain that my money would be invested through Bell Potter Securities. In order to get that rolling, I needed to fill in loads of paperwork, have my identity verified and open an investment account.

'And then what?'

'Once that's been verified, go to Westpac and get a bank cheque made out to Bell Potter Securities for the full amount.'

Over the next week and with my list of to-dos in hand, I actioned everything and kept Max in the loop.

'Don't forget you've still got that other little investment from before Christmas. What do you want to do with it? Do you want to take it out or reinvest it?'

'Look, I don't really want to transfer it back at the moment. Just reinvest it. I trust you.'

'Done. Oh, by the way, we finally found a new CEO. Guy named Tony.'

'You must be so relieved. How's Ana doing?'

'She's good. I actually think she's going to start working for me. Jules, who's been helping me out for a few years, wants to take a step back from handling my personal affairs and external clients. When I mentioned needing a replacement to Ana, she put her hand up.'

'The Dream Team lives on!' I joked.

Max went on to volunteer that he was going to pay her $200,000 a year, only slightly more than he'd been paying his sister. He also said that Ana would be across everything regarding my investments and that I could always reach out to her if I needed anything.

A multi-millionaire CEO resigns and becomes Max Tavita's personal assistant? In hindsight, I can see how this sounds odd. But at the time, I was so used to it being the 'Max and Ana' show that I didn't think twice about it. Plus, I was consumed by the task and promise of setting up my self-managed superfund.

Before hanging up, I reminded Max that we had dinner plans with my mum later that month and reconfirmed that he was still available.

'Yep. Wouldn't miss it.'

On 10 February 2017, I gave Max the bank cheque for Bell Potter Securities for $187,000.

In preparation for Mum's visit, I was busy getting my apartment ready and thinking about how happy, calm and abundant I felt. Was this the elusive light at the end of the tunnel that everyone kept telling me about when I'd first left Prince Charming? For so much of 2015, I'd felt like I was in the eye of a storm. But now, thanks to people like Max, I could see the clouds lifting and sunlight shining through. I felt loved, I felt secure and I felt empowered to create the life I'd been envisioning. My gratitude was only amplified when Mum arrived and made her famous

'Booty's Cheesecake' for Asha and me. What I'm saying is that my heart and stomach were both very full.

Since Mum hadn't seen Asha over Christmas, the majority of her visit was spent in Nanny Bootcamp mode. When Asha wasn't at school, they were building sandcastles at Freshwater Beach, putting in serious time at the playground and ensuring that no ice cream cones went unfinished. By the time Friday rolled around and we dropped Asha to her dad's, we were both knackered and really looking forward to adult time and dinner with Max. Even though they'd met when we'd been up north on the holidays, Mum was keen to spend some more quality time with him.

Unfortunately, she didn't get the chance. Late that afternoon, Max called to cancel our dinner plans because he had to work on some legal matters with the 'Foster Fam' parents at Narrabeen. I tried not to sound terribly disappointed, but it must not have worked. On his way to the legal meeting, Max turned up at my doorstep with two bottles of wine and two bouquets of flowers. Mum and I couldn't help but smile at the gesture.

'I'm so sorry I'm cancelling dinner. I promise we'll do it another time,' Max said vehemently.

Mum and I assured Max that he was forgiven before taking our wine and flowers inside. Mum asked me about Max's foster family and what legal matters he could possibly be helping them with. I knew that they ran a pretty successful handbag business, loved skiing and had taken Max under their wing as a teen, but didn't have much more information. The best I could come up with was that maybe they needed investment or financial help from Max. Knowing it really wasn't our business, we shrugged it off, went to dinner and spent most of the time talking about how I was finding being back at work, how Asha was adjusting to Year 1 and Max's idea that we all meet up in Byron Bay for Easter.

'A family Easter in Byron sounds great,' Mum said with delight.

'Max said he's going to send me some rental options this week. Would it be okay if we dropped Asha to you so we can have a few days on our own? You and Asha can come down on Tuesday or Wednesday and stay with us.'

'Happy to do that,' replied Mum, nursing a glass of wine. 'It sounds great.'

'Thanks Ma, you're the best. We can sort details down the track. I'm sure we'll get a place big enough for everyone. I'll touch base with the boys.'

Mum set her glass down and asked, 'Does Max flash his money around a lot?'

This came out of left field and I paused to consider my answer. 'In the beginning, I kind of felt like he did, but not really anymore. He pays for probably eighty per cent of the stuff we do, like accommodation and big dinners. But I make an effort to pay for meals here and there, pick up a bottle of wine or cook nice dinners for us.'

'I guess it would be weird for him not to pay for those bigger things if he has the type of money he says he has.'

I nodded. 'Yeah. He is very generous.'

The day after Mum left, I flipped our wall calendar to March. Where was the time going? Honestly, my five-month sabbatical felt like it was over in the blink of an eye and, in a way, like I was in the same place before I'd left. Overworked and overwhelmed, I was slightly irked that I hadn't figured out how to work more sustainably yet. At least I was clearer on what I wanted my future to look like and was just months away from finalising my divorce with Prince Charming. Trying not to be hard on myself for not completely transforming my life in less than a year, I dropped Asha to school and caught the bus to work. While en route, I got a text from Cath asking if we could meet for breakfast the next day. *I wonder what this is about.*

Cath and I caught up as much as we could but a pre-work breakfast was not the easiest of time slots to fill; especially for Cath who had two kids and a full-time job as a data partnerships lead for a content company. Within minutes of arriving at the cafe, I could tell our meeting was about something serious. As soon as we got past the 'How's work? How's the divorce? How are the kids?' chat, tears filled Cath's eyes. Cath never cries. Not even when I made her watch *Beaches*. *Please don't let it be cancer.*

In a trying-to-be-strong voice, Cath began to speak. 'Trace. I love you. So much. The last thing I want to do is lose you. But if I don't say this, I'll never forgive myself.'

Bracing for the worst, I leaned forward and nodded to let her know it was okay to continue.

'I'm really concerned about Max. I'm not sure he is who he says he is. And I'm worried about your money.'

Taken aback, it took me a few seconds to figure out what to say. 'Cath, you've never met him. I promise you don't need to be concerned.'

Cath, whose voice regained a bit of normalcy, asked, 'Have you seen his driver's licence? What about his credit cards?'

'No ...' I said in a semi-defensive tone.

Cath, who like me was ignoring her meal entirely, straightened up in her chair. 'I want you to go through his wallet and see if he really is "Max Tavita".'

'I would never do that. I'm not that type of person.' Even talking about snooping around made me feel icky. I reached for Cath's hands and held them tight. 'You just don't know him. Max is the most solid man I've ever known. You'll see when you meet him.'

'When can I meet him? That's the other thing ... He is always bailing on your plans that involve your friends.'

This point ruffled my feathers. It was true that Max rarely fronted up to a social plan involving my friends and family. Still, I felt like I needed to defend him. 'He's lived such a different life than us. And he works unusual hours. When it matters, he shows up. Did I tell you he's spending Easter with my family in Byron?' (No, the accommodation wasn't booked yet, but it felt like something I could grasp at.)

Cath didn't appear to be pacified by anything I was saying and within seconds, the tears were back. *Weird.*

'Look, I appreciate you looking out for me, but I trust Max – with my heart and my money. He's been there for me in ways I never could have imagined. Plus, he got me a one hundred per cent return on an investment I made last November.'

Cath raised her eyebrows. 'Nobody ever gets a one hundred per cent return on their money. Even ten per cent is unheard of.' Before I could respond, Cath took a deep breath and added, 'I really want to be wrong. With all my heart, I want Max to be who he says he is. I want you to be happy, in love and financially secure. And if he's getting one hundred per cent returns, then I want him to manage my superfund!'

That last remark made us both smile, which eased the tension.

'Look, I'm going to book a dinner so you can meet him. Cath, I promise you're going to love him.'

'Okay. Let me know where and when. I'm there.'

Cath and I had a long hug before heading to our offices. What Cath hadn't told me at this 'friendtervention' was that her spidey senses had turned her into an amateur sleuth who would have quite the dossier on the enigmatic 'Max Tavita' in the coming months.

CHAPTER 19

Big Dreams, Bigger Returns

Three weeks later, I was on a plane to Byron Bay, sipping soda water and writing to Max in my journal.

On my way to see you! Yippee. So damn excited to be spending the weekend with you. Have been wishing the hours away for the last few days and keeping busy so as not to think about it too much. I'm so happy you're having an awesome time up there. And so bloody stoked you love Byron as much as I do.

It's been killing me you being there this week without me … so jealous! Ha.

I get butterflies when I think about seeing you and being with you again. I have to be careful because I know that it won't be how I imagine it when we see each other. But we will be together and that's all that matters right now. Another week in Byron with you, my love. Can.not.wait.

Even though Max didn't want to make a fuss about his birthday, he did seem intent on going all out when it came to our accommodation. He wanted to be within walking distance to Wategos Beach so we could walk straight out the door to surf. We booked three nights at Victoria's at Wategos, a boutique hotel that boasts room rates even higher than Halcyon House. With work finally slowing down, Max decided to tack on an extra seven days and head up early with Chris. Max, the ever faithful shit-stirrer, had been sending me pics all week of them hanging at the beach, scoping out properties and drinking kombucha cocktails at The Roadhouse. By the time I'd arrived, Chris had flown home, which meant Max and I could get straight into doing our favourite things.

Just like many of our weekends in Bondi or Freshwater, the thing we loved most about being in a beachside town was catching the sunrise on our early morning walks, drinking coffee through lids that were wet with sea spray and listening to the waves crash in the middle of the night. Since this was now our third trip together to the area, we started fantasising about one day owning our own place. The fact that Max was seriously thinking about a future 'retired life' in Byron made me feel better about him deciding that a move to Freshwater would put him too far away from the city in the interim. *At least there is a 'some day'.*

On this trip we met Liam, a laidback but switched-on real estate agent, who'd later go on to show us numerous properties and provide multiple floor plans and contracts for us to review during our visits in April and July. One property that stood out was a luxury guesthouse close to the beach. Priced around $4.5 million, I was in disbelief that this was in Max's price range. Then again, he'd casually told me he'd sold his New York apartment for $24 million (and showed me a bunch of pictures and the listing). Plus, he was always sending me Bondi listings of more than $5 million that he was considering buying.

When we got tired of talking about houses, Max and I set off to the hinterland for a bite to eat at an incredible farm-to-table restaurant called Harvest in nearby Newrybar. Famous for being home to the late Olivia Newton-John's health retreat, Gaia, and a large portion of the Hemsworth brothers' real estate portfolio, Newrybar's quaint homes and rolling green hills reminded me of my time in the Lakes District during my gap years in the UK. Of course, the lack of stonework and abundance of cockatoo and kookaburra bird calls left little doubt that Newrybar was Australian through and through. That said, Harvest did serve up a lamb shoulder and glass of red that would transport anyone to an English hunting lodge – savoury, soft and satiating in every way. I was on the corner of Food Heaven and Food Coma.

Somehow, I found the strength to redirect my blood flow from my stomach to my brain so I could do some life planning. For weeks, I'd been trying to organise a time for us to have dinner with Cath and her husband Brendan, but Max had yet to give me any viable dates.

'Do you know when you're going to be free for dinner with Cath and Brendan? I really want you to meet them.'

Max, who looked every bit as lamb-shoulder drunk as I did, replied, 'Ah yes. Sorry, Bub. I keep forgetting to send you dates when I have my diary open. I promise I'll get them to you this week when I'm back at work.'

'You're going to love Cath. She's hilarious.'

'How'd you meet her again?'

'We worked together at AAPT when I got back from India and have been friends ever since. Cath's one of those extremely clever, well-read, successful, half-marathon-running mums who make life look effortless.'

'Like you.' Max winked.

I playfully rolled my eyes. 'Except for the whole half-marathon-running thing.'

Max smiled. 'She sounds awesome.'

'She totally is. Right, Mister, it's your birthday tomorrow – I'm thinking we drive to Halcyon House and eat at Paper Daisy. We know we love the food and we can reminisce about our first trip away.'

Max cocked his head. 'I don't know. It's kind of far and the weather is shit.'

Trying to help, I suggested we could get an Uber so we didn't have to drive.

Max shook his head. 'Nah, I don't trust anyone to drive me in this rain. I just want to relax, T. You're here with me. That's all that matters.'

'Come on. We've got to do something.'

'My actual birthday isn't even until Tuesday. How about I come over after work and we can do something with Jerry?'

Max's lack of birthday dinner enthusiasm was a bit deflating. I know forty-three isn't a milestone birthday but I had envisioned him blowing out birthday cake candles after a nice meal out. That is if Max was willing to eat birthday cake. From what I'd learned, even cake was too 'gooey' and calorific for him. On the flip side, I liked that he wanted to celebrate with Asha.

'Alright, fine, we'll do something chill for dinner. But tomorrow's surf session is a birthday surf session.'

Max leaned in to kiss me on my cheek. 'I can't think of a better gift.'

The next morning, Max and I agreed that we couldn't have asked for better conditions at Broken Head. Even though it required us to drive twenty minutes out of town, the waves were consistent and mellow for the whole session after we got in the water at 7 am. While I was audibly enjoying the fact that I was spending more time standing up than falling down, Max couldn't get over the fact that we were the only people there. At one point when we were both having a rest on our bellies on our boards, Max paddled his to be closer to mine and grabbed my hand.

After scanning my eyes and face for a few seconds, Max said, 'God, you're beautiful. Have I told you how much I love your blue eyes and gorgeous smile and bronzed skin?'

'Yes but I am open to hearing it again,' I replied before kissing his hand.

Max kissed mine back. 'This is the perfect life, T.'

'My only regret is that we didn't meet sooner. I would have loved to be doing life with you all these years,' I said.

Max sat up and straddled his board, which prompted me to follow suit. 'I know. Guess we'll just have to make up for lost time.' He turned and started paddling out. 'One more wave?'

'Yep. And then I need to eat.'

Max laughed. 'Definitely don't want to do life with hangry TT.'

On our way back to Victoria's, Max's petrol light reminded us that we'd been on 'empty' for longer than preferred. We pulled into a service station and after refuelling, Max started to walk inside to pay, but paused, turned back with his wallet open and asked, 'Do you have your card on you? I forgot to put money into this account.'

I looked in my bag but was confident I'd only packed my towel, change of clothes and sunscreen before heading out the door. I never take my purse or phone to the beach. 'Sorry, I don't have it on me.'

'All good. I just need to ring Ana and have her transfer some money.'

I glanced at the petrol pump and saw the total was $79.63. *That's weird. He doesn't even have $80 in his account?*

Because it was nearly 10 am and we hadn't eaten, my stomach didn't let me dwell on Max's account balance for too long. In fact, my stomach demanded most of my attention until we got changed back at the hotel and were sitting down to eat a short time later. As usual, Max ordered fully cooked eggs ('No runny bits, please') and very crispy, well-done bacon ('I don't want any soft fat'). When our food arrived, I awkwardly watched Max pull the clearly-not-cooked-enough fat and rind off the bacon and make a show of telling the waiter it wasn't how he'd ordered it.

For the majority of our time together, Max was always a truly decent human but on this trip, I couldn't help but think he was being a bit of a menace – especially to the owner, Victoria, at her namesake property. When I'd arrived in our room, he'd taken the throw off our bed and noticed a rip in the fabric. Deeming this unacceptable, he took it down to reception to complain. Look, I get that when you're paying over $1000 a night, you expect the best of the best, but everything he was upset about felt trivial.

When the waiter came back to clear our plates (and attempt to make amends), Max had thankfully transformed back into a humble and happy human. I insisted on paying the bill (mostly so I could leave an 'I'm sorry about my boyfriend' tip) and we slowly strolled back to our hotel. Max, who was cleaning his sunnies on his shirt, brought up my self-managed superfund. 'Your investment is going well. You've already made $23,000 in the last few weeks. If we keep going like this for a year, you are going to be so sweet, T.'

'Can you show me a monthly breakdown of what my super is doing? I want to keep on top of it.'

'Of course. I'll get it to you when we're back in Sydney. That reminds me, I'll do your tax return for 2015 to 2016 too. I just need a list of all your expenses.'

'Sure, I'll get that to you when I get home.'

'Have you thought about cashing in more of your eBay and PayPal shares and putting it in your superfund?'

I let out a sigh because, yes, I had thought about it but my gut made me think I should operate with a 'set and forget' mentality with those shares. However, the returns Max was getting for me and his clients made me think otherwise.

Max filled in the gap in our conversation. 'I only ask because you want to sell them while the US stock market is high, which it is right now, and before it crashes, which it will.'

At this point, I had done the mental maths (meaning I googled it on my phone while walking) and was under the impression that there had been a fifteen per cent increase since Max had started managing my money. I didn't think this was out of the ordinary because of the types of returns the family office got.

'Let me look into this a bit more when I'm back in Sydney. Leaning toward yes.'

Max put his arm around me. 'Smart cookie.'

•

On the morning of Max's actual birthday, Asha woke me up well before 6 am by using my face as a playground for her rainbow-coloured Beanie Boo lion. Wanting to do something sweet for Max, Asha and I didn't bother to wipe the sleep from our eyes or wait for the pillowcase imprints from our cheeks to fade before filming a video of us singing a very croaky and unrehearsed duet of 'Happy Birthday'. Just as we were singing the part where you say the person's name, Asha decided 'Monkey' sounded better than 'Max'.

After our 'hip hip hoorays' but with the camera still rolling, I asked, 'Why is he a monkey?'

'Because he's cheeky!' Asha exclaimed.

'He is cheeky … He's cheeky 'cos he calls you Jerry …'

Asha excitedly giggled. 'Happy birthday, Monkey!'

I laughed before wrapping up our virtual birthday card. 'We hope you have a great day and we can't wait to see you later.'

With her Beanie Boo in hand, Asha waved, 'Bye bye, Monkey!'

When 'Monkey' knocked on our apartment door roughly twelve hours later, Asha and I quickly flipped the lights off and lit the four candles we'd placed in the stack of the finest non-gooey chocolate-covered donuts we could get our hands on. Once ready, I stayed in the kitchen to film the surprise while Asha led Max into the kitchen with his right hand covering his closed eyes. We'd only sung the first two words of our now-rehearsed-once duet of 'Happy Birthday' when Max removed his hand to see what we'd been up to. Before his hand could even get to his waist, he was waving 'no' and taking a step back to hide behind a wall.

'No photos,' he said, sounding like the bodyguard of a celebrity.

Asha, who didn't seem fussed by Max's disappearing act, kept singing.

Max interjected, 'No photos!'

'I'm filming,' I tried to say in an upbeat tone to coax him in.

Reluctantly, Max faced his fear of cameras and joined us at the kitchen bench to listen to the rest of our performance. I don't know what switch he had to flip but he managed to give us a big, 'That's amaaaaaaaazing!' before blowing out his candles.

CHAPTER 20

Investing in Our Future

Because my eBay and PayPal shares had vested, cashing them in was quick and easy. So was getting the money to Max. Unlike when I'd written the $187,000 cheque to Bell Potter Securities, Max, who was spending a lazy Sunday at mine, instructed me to transfer the $80,000 I'd gotten for the shares into an account called 'OFM Client Account'.

Curious as to why the change, I asked, 'What is OFM? Why is it going there?'

'Oh, sorry. OFM is Oceania Financial Markets. It's a company I use to run the investments I handle outside of the family office. Because we're all set up now, I can invest the money that's in your super trading account easier this way.'

'No worries,' I replied. It took a few minutes to make the transfer.

In retrospect, I should have looked up the company on the ASIC website. Because then I would have seen it was in his sister Jules's name and asked why. But let's be honest – Max would have given some seemingly plausible reason.

Even though I was fully confident in Max's thinking and trusted him wholeheartedly (and was not thinking about ASIC at all), I did have a few concerns about what would happen to my money if, god forbid, something were to happen to him. Aside from receiving the email daily market reports he sent all his clients, I had yet to see a statement or summary from Max regarding my SMSF.

'Oh, one more thing. Can I have the login details for my trading accounts and all the investments you're making with my super?'

Max, who was lying on my lounge in the opposite of life-admin mode, casually replied, 'Yeah, I can get all that to you, but you won't need it.'

Because my back was toward Max, I spun around in my chair and said, 'I'm just a bit worried. I know this sounds horrible, but what if …'

Max finished my sentence. 'If I die?'

'Yeah, I don't have anything on file. I don't know any of the logins. I've been asking you for them.'

In a reassuring voice, Max said, 'Bub, I'm one step ahead of you. Remember, this is not a friend favour I'm doing, it's a business I run. Don't worry, Ana is my power of attorney and handles all of my affairs. There's processes and procedures in place for this type of thing so you'd get a phone call from Ana.'

'Yeah, but I don't even have Ana's number.'

Max, who was now walking over to me for a cuddle, replied, 'Don't worry – it's all in hand.'

Now wrapped in Max's arms, I gently teased, 'But I don't know any of this.'

'It's all good, T. Don't stress. I'll make sure you get all the details.'

•

With our Easter trip just days away, Max and I were both working our butts off to wrap everything up before heading up the coast. At eBay, I was busy running multiple campaigns and trying to connect with a new boss, while ensuring I was also delivering high value customers. Max, who was already feeling the end-of-financial-year tax pressure, one-upped my long workdays by pulling multiple all-nighters in the city. He had so much additional work on his plate that in those last seventy-two hours before our holiday, pretty much the only way we connected was via his weekly email update.

This update was intended for family office client eyes only, but Max frequently forwarded them to me. It sometimes felt like I was reading another language, but I enjoyed getting a glimpse into Max's world ... especially when he was too busy for our regular meetups. Each update typically featured a general overview of how the ASX 200 and NASDAQ-100 were performing, before diving into a play-by-play of the trades the family office had made. More often than not, their moves proved very profitable. But every now and then, Max would humbly admit when they'd missed an opportunity or copped a decline. Of course, this news was always followed by words of wisdom and a plan of action.

Perhaps I liked reading these email updates so much because they reassured me that my money was in safe and intelligent hands. It was nice knowing my boyfriend was a finance nerd. However, I really hoped Max would park the 'bullish market' talk by the time Asha and I met up with him in Byron. I had tried to convince Max to fly with us but, like all the other times, he insisted on having his ute and all his surfboards with him at Byron Bay. Even though driving felt like wasting two days of our time off, it was nice not to have to travel with oversized items.

Instead of enjoying bouts of comfortable silence, singing along to Tori Amos and making Max listen to Chelsea Handler's stand-up comedy routine, I spent the flight to Byron being a literal captive audience for Asha, who evidently had no shortage of stories, fun facts, opinions, musings and ideas that *needed* to be shared. She was (and always has been) a great travel buddy but, needless to say, I was grateful for the adult time Max and I got to have once we'd dropped Asha to my mum.

As much as I enjoyed getting to be 'just us' for a few days, my truly favourite part of this trip was the time that Max and I spent with my family and friends. Mum and Asha stayed with us, while my brother Marty came down for a day of surfing and hot chips on the beach between

Clarkes and The Pass. We were joined by our old school friends, Jen and Rich, as well as Gareth and his kids. Together, we set up our base camp with much-needed large umbrellas to block the sun and a swag of beach towels for us to collapse on. The weather was amazing, as was Max's energy, generosity and patience. Without being asked, he'd organised board rentals for the kids and gathered more beach toys than you could poke a stick at.

After pushing the kids onto waves for hours, we came up for sustenance and sandcastle building. Clearly keen to really rip in, Max and Rich headed off for bigger thrills. First, they caught a few waves on longboards but pretty quickly they swapped to shortboards as they dodged the scuba boats that were heading out to Julian Rocks. Sunshine, waves, friends, family, Max … I don't think I've ever been happier. The sun stayed high in the sky the entire day and, like us, lingered for hours before heading home for the night. As much as I loved living in Freshwater, this day in particular made me wonder if Max and I could expedite our dream of moving to Byron.

The rest of our trip was much the same. Beach, surf, hot chips … rinse and repeat. Every now and then Max locked himself away in the study to work but for the most part, he was happily pushing Asha onto waves, playing board games with us or whipping up nibbles with the supplies Mum and I had picked up from the farmers market. Mum could also see how much we loved this little pocket of Australia, especially when she and Asha accompanied us on some walk-throughs and drive-bys of a few hinterland properties that were for sale with Liam.

Our favourite was a jaw-dropping property just ten minutes from the heart of Byron. Expected to go for over $4 million, it was nestled in green rolling hills and offered the type of ocean views that take your breath away.

'Just a simple home for three,' I joked.

Mum whispered under her breath to me, 'Four. I'm moving here with you.'

Max, who had clearly mastered his real estate poker face, playfully rolled his eyes at our blatant excitement while peppering Liam with questions about the quality of the build and the terms of the contract. Like many of the other homes we'd inspected, this one had the potential to be Airbnb'd when we weren't staying there. On the drive back to Byron, we talked about the different ways we could buy it. Max thought it made the most sense to do it through one of our self-managed superfunds or as a company. This conversation reminded me that I still hadn't received a statement of how my fund was performing. Not wanting to chat about it in front of Mum, Asha or Liam, I changed the subject and decided to come back to it when we were home in Sydney.

From the moment we returned after our holiday, I couldn't stop thinking about how Max and I could own a home together in Byron one day. Knowing I didn't want it to be something he bought for us, I wanted to map out a savings and investments plan. (Clearly, I'm Type A.) As a lover of spreadsheets and someone who always has at least ten tabs open on my work computer to review marketing budgets and projections, I wanted to do the same with my personal finances. Annoyingly, I still didn't have my account login information or even a report from Max. Again, I pressed him for something I could work with.

> Tracy: Hey, I meant to ask you last night – can you send me the login details for my super account and can we go through it this weekend at some point to help me understand how it all works? Xx
> Max: Of course. Had it planned. xx

Due to the business of life and the fact that I was planning a surprise mother–daughter trip for Mum's seventieth birthday, I didn't notice when a month had gone by and I still hadn't received any information from Max. Irritated but not concerned, I set off with my mum to tick a huge item off her bucket list: Uluru. Knowing it was somewhere she'd always wanted to go, I couldn't wait to experience it with her. We'd actually travelled to Vietnam together not long after Dad died and it was amazing. At sixty years old, she had thrown on an old backpack of mine and said, 'Yes, let's do it!' Booty is a bloody legend.

Neither of us had been to the centre of Australia before and were in awe of just how red the dirt was and how magnetic Uluru felt. While watching the sunrise over the desert, Mum and I chatted about how much Dad would have loved it. My heart hurt thinking about how long she'd been on her own. Even though Mum had dated a little bit, she hadn't managed to find another Snugglepot to her Cuddlepie. Eventually, the conversation turned to Max and me.

'Does Max want kids?' Mum asked.

To be honest, we actually haven't spoken about it.

'I'm not sure. He hasn't said he wants kids. And I think he knows I feel complete with Asha.' At forty-one, I'd come to terms with the fact I probably wouldn't have any more children. It was just the way things had worked out. (The witch doctor in Nepal with his prediction of two boys and two girls was way off the mark.)

Mum nodded. 'I was wondering because he really is so great with kids. I loved watching him in the surf with Asha.'

'Me too,' I said while wistfully imagining coming back to Uluru with Max one day.

A few days after I got back from my trip with Mum, Max arrived at my place with a fourteen-page report from Bell Potter Securities. While I read through the official statement, Max poured a glass of wine and placed it in my hand. I could see the name of my fund followed by pages of lines listing trades with other funds.

'What do these figures mean?' I asked, pointing to a column on the right.

Max peered over my shoulder and explained, 'Those won't mean much on their own ... they're just the individual trades with different funds.'

Max took the report from my hands and flipped to the last page before pointing to a bold bottom number: $394,000.00.

'That's the number you should care about. That's what your fund is currently worth.'

Seeing as I'd only put in $267,000 over the course of three months, $394,000 seemed incredible. *See, Cath – you didn't need to worry about me.*

CHAPTER 21

Party of Four

It took nearly three months to get in the diary, but Max and I were *finally* having dinner with Cath and her husband, Brendan, in early June at Cho Cho San in Potts Point. Just like when Max was going to meet Kelly, I found myself hoping that Cath and Max would love each other just as much as I loved each of them. I wanted Max to see that just because he was a non-gooey 'vanilla' type of guy, that didn't mean that he couldn't socialise with my extremely gooey 'rainbow sprinkles' bestie. I also wanted Cath to lay to rest the idea that Max was trying to pull a fast one on me.

Max and I arrived uncharacteristically early and were told our table wasn't quite ready. As I idly waited by the front door, catching a chill up my dress every time someone went in or out, I watched Max silently 'clear the room' like usual. It didn't matter if we were meeting in a cafe, conference room or cocktail bar, Max *always* had to mentally take note of the people and, most importantly, check for the exits. *Because of 9/11.* I understood why he felt hypersensitive in crowded public spaces but it always felt a bit like a boy playing a make-believe game of *Special Ops.*

By the time Max had given Cho Cho San the 'all-clear', Cath and Brendan were making their way through the door. Cath was in her best dress while Brendan was swaddled in an oversized brown jumper. Cath and I hugged hello while Max and Brendan went in for a handshake. When it was time to swap partners (not in the keys-in-a-fishbowl kind of way), Cath threw her arms around Max, pulled him in *very* close and said how thrilled she was to finally meet the elusive Max Tavita. Max's beaming smile and apology for taking so long to book in our dinner felt genuine. I did still wonder if he was simultaneously looking for any exits he may have missed.

Within minutes of being shown to our table, it was clear that Cath had brought 'extra sprinkles AND whipped cream on top' energy and had more than just double-date plans in mind. Bubbly, engaged and firing off questions as if leading a coronial inquest, Cath was evidently on a mission to *really know* the man who had stolen my heart.

'Max! Trace mentioned your offices are at 1 Bligh Street.'

Max had his hand on my leg. 'That's right,' he replied.

'It's an incredible piece of real estate. Do you ever see the prime minister?'

'I've yet to cross paths with Malcolm but certainly see a lot of other politicians hanging about.'

'When did you start leasing there? Did you ever see Julia Gillard?'

'No, we came in about two years after she resigned.'

'So many high-profile people at 1 Bligh! You probably can't say … but who are some of your clients?'

Max cheekily replied, 'You're right. I can't really say.'

Cath, who could easily work for the CIA, pressed harder. 'Oh, come on! This is a safe space.'

Max hesitated before replying. 'Alright. I'm not saying these are our clients, but we work with people like the Murdochs, Gerry Harvey and the Pratt family.'

Just as Max was opening his mouth to ask a question, Cath cut in. 'Tell me about your time with NASA. You worked on algorithms or something? Trace says you're a mathematical genius.'

Max gave my leg a little squeeze. 'Trace is being too kind. Technically, I worked for Lockheed Martin. I helped develop and finesse their heat-seeking missile technology.'

'That's incredible. And you went to MIT, right?'

'Yeah, I spent sixteen years in the US before taking time off to cycle through Europe.'

'Brendan goes mountain biking all the time,' Cath offered.

Max turned to Brendan. 'Where do you like to ride?'

Brendan's face lit up. 'All over the place, but the Blue Mountains have some great trails.'

Max smiled. 'Nice. We should ride together sometime. I don't mountain bike much – mostly road biking.'

'That would be great,' Brendan said. 'I've been meaning to dust off my old road bike … Trace said you raced triathlons quite a bit.'

'Yeah, for a few years.'

Cath let out a gasp of excitement. 'Oh! You must know our family friend, Annabel Luxford.'

Max squinted his eyes trying to match the name to a face before shaking his head no.

Cath, who looked like she was making a mental note that Max didn't know Annabel, replied, 'Really? She's a world champion triathlete. Even represented Australia at the Commonwealth Games.'

Max was drawing a blank. Brendan eased the awkwardness by asking for Max's number so they could tee up a ride sometime.

Midway through dinner, Cath leaned across the table and used her fork to swipe a piece of chicken from Max's plate. 'You don't mind if I try some, do you?'

Seeing as we'd already had the discussion that our shared entrees couldn't be 'gooey' and that the sauces needed to be on the side, Cath knew very well how fastidious Max was about his food. And because she had heard me talk about his need to shower before and after sex as well as his need for excessive hand washing, I watched the rest of this interaction unfold with bated breath.

'I don't mind.' (His words may have said he didn't but his skin conductance said he did.)

'Thanks, I just love Cho Cho San's chicken so much. We probably should have ordered two serves.'

Cath swallowed, wiped her face with a serviette and then – no joke – reached across the table and picked up Max's drink. Without seeking *any* sort of consent, she took a sip and then placed it back down in front of him. 'I think I'm going to order one of those.'

The look on Max's face made me think his death was imminent and I didn't want to witness it.

'And I think I'm going to go to the toilet!' Even though I was actually kind of curious to see if Max would spontaneously combust, I really did have to pee.

A few minutes later, Cath's head was looking down at me from the top of the bathroom stall partition. 'Can you believe I took a sip of his drink?'

I laughed. 'You're so cheeky! He'd be dying right now!'

'I know. I love it.'

'So, what do you really think?' I asked while pulling up my knickers.

'I think he clearly adores you.'

'Thank you. But what do you think about him as a person?'

'I think he comes across as nice, charming and intelligent.'

I joined Cath at the sink to wash my hands and made eye contact with her in the mirror. With a smile, I said, 'He really is. I'm so excited – we just booked another trip to Byron. We're going next month because I've been asked to speak at a women's event about marketing on the Gold Coast.'

'You two treat Byron like it's your weekender.'

'Ha! I wish we could buy a weekender there. We've actually been looking at a few properties. Max is more serious than I am, though … he sends me listings all the time.'

Cath raised her eyebrows. 'Make sure you buy something with room for me.'

I laughed and led the way back to the table. The rest of dinner still felt like Max was sitting down for an in-depth interview. Cath had morphed into Barbara Walters and managed to touch on his parents' plane crash, his fleet of cars and his ex-fiancée. Max, who only managed to squeeze a few questions in for Cath and Brendan, seemed to have an answer for everything.

After saying goodbye and getting into an Uber back to his place, I asked Max what he thought of Cath. Much to my delight, Max said he got a kick out of Cath and enjoyed Brendan's company.

'She's a character, that's for sure. But why was Brendan wearing a big woolly grandpa jumper?'

Taken aback by the snide remark, I came to Brendan's defence. 'It's cold out! Plus, that jumper is a classic.'

Max was now half-paying attention to me and half-checking his phone. 'I think it ages him.'

Says the guy wearing drop-crotch pants in a desperate attempt to look ten years younger ...

•

The following weekend, I woke to find Max working on his laptop in my kitchen.

'Babe, it's Sunday,' I said, wiping the sleep from the corners of my eyes.

'I know. But I just have so much end-of-financial-year stuff to get through.'

I gave him a look of sympathy before boiling the kettle. 'Do you want coffee?'

'Yes but not …'

'I know, I know. Not *my* coffee. I'll duck out to Pilu.'

While slipping on my shoes and jacket, I thought about how incredible it was that I'd managed to sleep until 8.30 am. 'Be back in ten,' I said, closing the screen door behind me.

As soon as I stepped onto the footpath, I spotted one of my best friends, Pene, on the footpath next to Max's car. (FYI, her name is pronounced as 'penny', not as the pasta or appendage.)

'Well, this is a fun surprise! What are you doing in my neck of the woods?'

I walked over and gave Pene a hug. Pene reached into her pocket, pulled out a $20 note and said, 'Sorry it's so early. I'm meeting some school mums for breakfast and thought I'd drop in with that money I owe you for those Lorna Jane leggings.'

'Aw, thanks. You didn't have to do that.'

'No, no. I want you to have it. What are you up to today?'

I told Pene that I was grabbing coffees for Max and me and that he was deep in end-of-financial-year work. Pene, whose husband worked in finance, sympathised before saying, 'Cath said she got to meet Max! Said he was really nice. I hope I get to meet him soon too.'

'You will! Just need to get through June.'

With that, I kissed Pene goodbye, picked up our coffees and returned to my apartment. Max was right where I'd left him. After taking the ristretto from my hands, and in among other chitchat about the surf, what we were going to do that day and if I'd bought the papers, Max asked me if I had any other money I'd consider putting into my self-managed superfund.

Thinking about the bonus I'd just gotten at work, I replied, 'I do ... why?'

'Asking because you could take advantage of a substantial tax break if you make a contribution before 30 June.'

'Really?'

'Yeah, if you're planning on investing more in the near future, you'd be silly not to do it before the end of the financial year. You can top your super up anytime you want.'

On 12 June 2017, I transferred $40,000 to an account named OFM Client.

CHAPTER 22

The Last Month

Aside from the printout that Max showed me of how my self-managed superfund was performing a month earlier, I had yet to receive formal documentation and needed it in order to finalise my divorce. Feeling bad about pestering Max when he was in the thick of end-of-financial-year work, I sent him a text on 28 June instead of calling.

> Tracy: QQ – do you have that statement on my super for my legal stuff?
>
> Max: Yes, can print any time.
>
> Tracy: Can you email? Just want to send to my lawyers to see whether it's what they need.

Because it was a Wednesday, Max planned to come to mine that night. And because my day took a turn for the worse shortly after I hit send on my last text, Max showed up and was immediately forced to listen to my rant about how unhappy I was at work (again) and that all I really wanted was to focus on getting ready for my presentation in Burleigh Heads on the Gold Coast.

'T, just quit,' Max said before lying down in 'his spot' on my lounge.

In a tone snappier than I intended, I replied, 'I can't *just* quit.'

Gracie hopped up on Max and lay down on his chest. Expecting him to shoo 'The Rat' away, I was taken aback when he let her curl up just inches from his face. 'Bub, I've made you your salary for the year in one week. You can leave work at any time.'

Still on the defence, I pointed out that my super was for 'future me' and that I couldn't live off those funds now. Max could have been trying to make a strong point or he could have reached his limit with Gracie, but he stood up and walked over to me in the kitchen. Wrapping me in his arms, Max said, 'You know I want nothing more than for you to be financially independent. You work so hard … Harder than anyone I know, actually.'

I nuzzled into Max's chest and let myself melt a bit. Sometimes, you just need someone to see how hard you're trying. Max took a step back and held my shoulders as if to get a good look at me. After a few seconds of staring deeply into my eyes, he walked around the bench and took a seat on a stool. 'What if I put one million dollars in your account tomorrow? You can take time off … actual time off. That five months was nothing. Take a year or two and see what you can do with your public speaking. Trace – you're such a gun when it comes to branding and marketing.' Max added, 'You can pay me back. I know you'd feel funny about it if it was a gift.'

The ego-stroking felt good but Max's $1 million proposal did not. Similar to the time he offered to buy me an around-the-world first-class plane ticket, this gesture felt like he was trying to 'save me' in a Sugar Daddy way I just really wasn't comfortable with. Plus, how was I ever going to pay back a million dollars? He was clearly living in a completely different reality than me.

'That's a really nice offer but I know I'm just having a bad day and am feeling stressed about speaking to a hundred people on the Goldie next week.'

Max stood and hugged me again. 'You're going to be fantastic. And remember, as soon as you're done – it's you, me and Byron beach walks.'

Grateful to have Max's (emotional) support, I powered through the rest of the work week feeling much more hopeful. Not only did I have the prospect of one day creating my own financial security to look forward to, I had one of my besties Emily's fortieth to look forward to that weekend. Unlike our twenty-firsts and thirtieths, which were celebrated with pure debauchery, Em had opted to celebrate her fortieth with an intimate private dinner at an incredible Italian restaurant in the city called Uccello. Seeing as this had been in the diary for months and I *really* wanted Max to meet Emily, I was less than thrilled when Max cancelled two days before Em's birthday. Citing 'family commitments', he wasn't going to be able to make it. Feeling terrible, I called Em, who assured me it would be fine. She'd just need to let Uccello know to shuffle the seating arrangements around.

Obviously, I would have preferred to be there with Max, but I will say that the chats I had with her cousin, a whip-smart and clever corporate lawyer, were top-notch. Apparently, he had been working on a big case with an Australian fashion designer he couldn't name.

Little did I know, this corporate lawyer would have definitely known who Max was … Turns out, the Australian fashion designer who couldn't be named was Lisa Ho – a woman who had trusted Max to manage her superfund. Perhaps Max had done some digging and suspected there might be people at the party who would blow his cover.

As usual, Max had more than one reason why he didn't want to fly with me when it was time to go up to Byron for our winter getaway and my presentation. Knowing I would spend my airport and plane time practising my speech, I didn't really care about Max opting for a road trip. Apparently, he had a few extra days up his sleeve so he headed up early and worked remotely. As long as he picked me up from the airport and stayed by my side in the surf, it didn't matter how or when he got there.

Since I'd arrived two days before I was due to present, Max and I spent our first morning together inspecting a fully renovated cottage on Massinger Street. Liam had mentioned this five-bedroom, three-bathroom, two-car garage property to us in May. It was perfect – drenched in light and what boho-chic dreams are made of. *How have we not been here already?!*

'What did Liam say this will go for again?' I whispered to Max.

'Three mil.'

'It's incredible. I could very much see us living here.'

'Imagine the parties Asha would have in the granny flat in high school.'

'We'll have to import Nanny Bootcamp for those years,' I said with a laugh.

'How is your mum, by the way?'

'She's good. Keeping busy with her volunteer work. I think she's going to meet us in Burleigh for dinner after my presentation on Saturday.'

'Nice. I still feel bad about cancelling dinner the last time she was down.'

'It's okay. Honestly. Oh, Rich and Jen are going to come too. Do you want to hang with Rich while I'm doing the presso? Jen's going to come and support me.'

'Yeah, I'll ask if he's keen for a surf.'

Ever since having dinner with Cath, Max and I had been having quite a few chats about making an effort to spend more time with each other's friends and families. I explained that it was normal for two people who have been seeing each other for over twelve months to be introduced to each other's significant friends and family. The reason I hadn't pushed it was because he seemed so resistant, and I was trying to respect his boundaries. However, it was getting to a point where now it was a big deal and it just didn't have to be. The fact that he was so keen to see Mum and my friends made me feel good but what I really wanted was for us to be spending time with his.

'Have you seen enough?' Max asked while squeezing my hand.

I let out a long sigh. 'Yep. It's perfect and I think we should buy it. Please and thank you.'

'I'll have my people get in touch with your people,' Max replied playfully.

For the rest of that day and night, I pretty much did nothing but practise and prepare for my presentation. Not to stroke my own ego, but I was pretty fantastic on the day. (No-one was falling asleep, okay!) In all seriousness, shortly after Max dropped me off at the venue, I spoke to an incredible group of women about how I handle my work-life 'mash-up'. As someone who has openly never believed in the work–life balance narrative, I gave practical examples and solutions of how I manage my career and single mummyhood at the same time. Because my background was in marketing, I spent a good portion of time speaking about the power and art of personal branding. Sure, I got to geek out about this stuff at work and with my friends, but there was something about getting to guide and inspire entrepreneurs and small business owners that really lit me up inside. I've always loved the emotive aspects of brand storytelling and there's nothing quite like getting to help someone dig deep to find the true heart and soul of who they are and the life they want to create.

After the conference finished and we were on the way to Rick Shores in Burleigh with Mum, Rich and Jen, I was still buzzing and thinking of how I could incorporate more speaking gigs into my life. Unless they were being held in Sydney, scheduled during out-of-work hours and somehow happening when I didn't have Asha, I just couldn't see how it was feasible. And so, I placed that dream on the backburner and focused on the dream right in front of me – Max. *How had I scored such a great guy? I wonder what story we'll write together.*

Hopefully, it was going to be one that featured many Sunday mornings just like the one we had on our final day of this trip. The weather was a chilly ten degrees when we woke up, which confirmed our plan of delaying surfing until after lunch. Bundled in flannel shirts, jumpers and beanies, we willed ourselves out the door to take advantage of our last beach walk for the holiday. While watching the sunrise and scrunching sand between our toes, we spoke at length about what would actually need to happen for us to live happily ever after in Byron and in Sydney. While I was more interested in hearing about how Max wanted to create a family unit with Asha and me, Max was keen to speak in detail about my investments and how I could use offshore accounts to minimise my taxes and fees even further.

'It's something you should consider, T. Think about it.'

Pretty sure the only time I'd used the term 'offshore account' in a sentence was when I was describing the plot of *The Firm* to a friend, I asked him what I'd have to do to set one up.

'That's my job, Bub. Leave that bit to me. All you'd need to do is think of a name that means something to you but can't obviously be traced to you … if you know what I mean.'

'Sounds dodgy.'

'I promise it's not. It's not what the ATO prefers but it's not technically illegal.'

'I'll think about it.'

Admittedly, I didn't get to think about much other than coffee, bacon and egg rolls and the final surf session we squeezed in before Max dropped me at the airport. As I didn't have much annual leave left, I left on Sunday while Max had the luxury of road-tripping home solo the following day. After kissing each other goodbye and saying 'I love you', I headed to my gate and waited to board. As I sat there people-watching, I thought about how grateful I was. Never had I felt more supported and secure with someone before. My mind went to the many profiles I'd had to swipe through to get to Max Tavita's. Thank goodness I hadn't given up. I journalled for the rest of the flight, mostly writing all the things I wanted to say to Max.

Well, it's taken me over a year to get to this point, but I am completely and totally smitten with you and with us. I still get butterflies every time I know I'm going to see you and get disappointed when I'm not. I love being with you and hanging out. I love the way you think about me and communicate with me. You're very thoughtful and careful with me. I love knowing our future together is something you want as well.

I'm happy with you in my life.

Def head over heels in love with you xx

●

When my plane touched down in Sydney, there was just enough daylight left for me to pick up Asha from her dad's and restock our fridge before prepping for the upcoming week.

Max and I exchanged a few texts before saying goodnight. The pesky restless leg syndrome I experience from time to time tried to prevent me from sleeping, but dreams of Byron Bay real estate were calling. When I woke at 6 am, I rang Max to see how his drive back to Sydney was going. Apparently, he'd left at 4 am, was listening to nothing but Kings of Leon and Powderfinger, and was planning to go into the office for a few hours before heading home. The mum that I am couldn't help but tell him to take it easy and not push too hard. Max playfully said, 'I know, I know.' Then we said goodbye.

The rest of the day flew by and before I knew it, Asha and I were drinking hot chocolate in matching pyjamas. Asha was anxious to know when she would see Max again. I said we'd probably do another big trip to Byron Bay for the summer school holidays. Asha's eyes lit up and she asked if she could go surfing again.

'Of course, darling. Max will push you on as many waves as you want,' I said dreamily. I carried our mugs to the sink before tucking Asha into bed. Knowing I wasn't too far behind, I gave Max a quick call to say goodnight.

'You're still at work?' I asked, glancing at the time. 'It's nearly 9 pm.'

Max let out a long sigh. 'I know. I've been up since three, so it's not ideal, but the new CEO is clearly still finding his feet.'

I knew mothering Max into going home wouldn't help. We exchanged I love yous, and I told him I was looking forward to our usual Wednesday date. He was too.

The next morning, I saw that a text from Max had come through at 1.37 am.

Max: Work work work xx

Due to the chaotic nature of single parenting during the school holidays, I didn't get a chance to respond and missed Max's call that came just after 8 am. By 7 pm that night, I realised we hadn't been able to connect all day. That was unusual to say the least.

Had something horrible happened to Max?

PART III

AFTER

'You can't connect the dots looking forward; you can only connect them looking backwards. So you have to trust that the dots will somehow connect in your future. You have to trust in something – your gut, destiny, life, karma, whatever. This approach has never let me down, and it has made all the difference in my life.'

STEVE JOBS

2005 Commencement Speech at Stanford University

Are You There Google? It's Me, Tracy

On 12 July 2017, my life quickly went from fact to fiction. My eyes didn't want to believe what they were seeing, no matter how many times I forced them to take in the online footage. The man I loved had been led away from his apartment in handcuffs the previous morning. And his name wasn't Max Tavita.

From the moment the words 'Who the fuck is Hamish?' left my mouth, the plagues began. Okay, so (Fresh)water didn't turn to blood and I wasn't batting locusts away. I was, however, living in a world of perpetual darkness and desperately trying to not drown in the flood of questions that were rising in my mind. Chris, who was (apparently) every bit as confused by the fact I thought my boyfriend's name was Max Tavita, couldn't get me off the phone quickly enough as I paced the footpath in front of my office. Offering me nothing other than the fact that Hamish sometimes went by Hamish Watson or Hamish McLaren, Chris never took a phone call from me again and didn't even have the decency to respond to text messages.

Wondering how on earth Chris and I could have possibly missed the contradicting names, I replayed my introduction and interactions with him. There'd been the first time we'd met at Max's, I mean Hamish's, apartment. As I tried to recount the small talk and farewell, it dawned on me: no-one ever said his name, including myself. Whenever I needed Max's attention, all I had to do was say, 'Babe'. Then I remembered the time in March when Chris was in Byron with Max staying at Victoria's before I arrived. Because it was such a small hotel with personalised service, the manager and customer service team went out of their way to call us 'Tracy' and 'Max' all weekend. It dawned on me that given the booking was under 'Max', the staff would have been using his name in front of Chris too. *Did he not say anything or ask any questions? Was this not odd for him? Did Hamish explain it away saying Ana had booked the hotel under this pseudonym? Perhaps Hamish was hoodwinking Chris too?* Finally, one last time popped into my head when Max and Chris threw some balls with my brother and his kids at the cricket nets near Kingscliff. My nephews would have definitely been calling him Max in front of Chris. *Was 'Max' an old nickname, one that wouldn't raise suspicions?*

When you think about it, we don't actually say someone's name very often, do we? And if you're Australian, it's possible that you don't even know their actual name because of our love of nicknames. And let's not forget, Max had about five nicknames for everyone. Aside from Asha's 'Monkey', the only time I ever heard anyone use a nickname for Max was when I briefly met one of the 'Foster Fam' boys, Matty, at his apartment. When Matty was leaving, he'd called Max 'Hambone'. After he left, I asked, 'Why Hambone?' and Max replied without taking a breath, 'I was really small and skinny at school and the kids told me my legs looked like bare ham bones. It just stuck.'

I can't tell you how long I stood frozen on the footpath having thoughts like these. I do, however, remember staring at my phone screen and realising I was having trouble getting my body to do pretty much anything. Part of me wanted to furiously google, call, text and figure out what was happening, while the other part wanted to shove it all into a nice neat little box, take the lift up to my office and pretend that everything was business as usual. Surely this was all just one big misunderstanding; a blip on the radar.

It could have been two or twenty minutes, but when I came out of what appeared to be a trance, I was relieved that I could feel my arms and legs and wiggle my fingers. Was that a stroke? I tapped my cheeks and made faces to make sure there hadn't been any lasting paralysis. Knowing that even IKEA wouldn't have enough products to compartmentalise the emotional turmoil I was experiencing, I called my colleague and friend Amber and told her what I knew. Within minutes, she had me slowly sipping water at a nearby cafe while we relayed to each other every piece of information we could find online about 'Hamish McLaren', 'Hamish Watson' and, after discovering yet another alias, 'Hamish Maxwell'.

The first thing we found was an article from 2003 that said 'Hamish Philip McRae Watson' lost his ASIC licence after being found guilty of stealing $5 million from Harts Australasia, a Brisbane accountancy group that had raised $30 million from investors and listed on the stock market in May 2000. Not only did Hamish allegedly funnel the money directly into his own accounts but his poor investments ultimately caused the group's collapse in October 2001 after posting a $93 million loss. The saddest part about the whole thing was that the group was made up of mum and dad investors who lost their life savings while Hamish walked away relatively unscathed and slithered off to Canada.

For over an hour, Amber and I read news article after news article chronicling the plethora of allegations made against Hamish. *Holy fuck, holy fuck, holy fuck.* As we continued to collect breadcrumbs, we eventually landed on a whole baguette when we found a website called hamishmcclaren.blogspot.com. Consisting of just four posts penned by an anonymous author, this little blog gave me my first glimpse into the magnitude of damage that Hamish had left in his wake over the last twenty years. It also made me realise that Hamish had been lying about way more than just his name. The first post had been published just three months earlier. It listed nine aliases before describing Hamish as a criminal who posed as a hedge fund manager with the alleged help of the Risk Advisory Group. The post also linked to a 2014 article by Hannah Low with the headline 'Lisa Ho recoups losses from former friend', published in the *Australian Financial Review*. According to the article, Hamish had stolen $850,000 from the Australian fashion designer in a superannuation scam. If only Hamish had gone to Emily's fortieth with me ... the corporate lawyer representing Lisa would have seen him and could have told me. *If only.*

Another link led to a 2002 *Sydney Morning Herald* article titled 'Show us the money, ASIC tells trader', about Hamish's role in the Harts Australasia scam. The journalist detailed that Hamish frequented A-list parties in the eastern suburbs, and had bought himself three Ferraris, two four-wheel drives and a motor cruiser in the space of a few weeks back in 2000. While I was working to reconcile that image with the man I knew, my mind was thrown into an even bigger tailspin when I read that Hamish had paid four million dollars for a house in Palm Beach and was often seen with TV personality Gabrielle Richens, also known as 'The Pleasure Machine'.

Where did the money come from? This question wasn't too hard to answer. It came from the pockets of unsuspecting Harts Australasia investors. But the many other questions that came up from reading the rest of the article have me still pondering the answers to this day. *Since when did he party with A-listers in the Eastern Suburbs? When did he live in Canada? Did he really own five properties including a house he built for $1.15 million near the Okanagan ski fields? He'd mentioned doing a* *ski season in Canada and shown me pictures, but never mentioned entering the real estate market abroad.*

How did he afford to pay the suburb record for a Palm Beach home ($3.9 million) in 1999? Did he ever live in New York? Did he really defraud victims in Great Britain and the Middle East?

But the most puzzling question was: *how could the person I just spent nearly two years of my life with seem to be almost the exact opposite to the one portrayed in the article?*

By the time I was strong enough to graduate from water to coffee, Amber and I followed a link from a third blog post that showed a 2016 legal document titled: 'Bankrupt Estate of Hamish McLaren'. As my eyes scanned the pages, I saw that Hamish had been born in 1970, not 1974. Shaving four years off your life is weird but not alarming. It was when I got to *Associated Entities* that the heart palpitations began. Out of the twelve associated companies listed, one jumped off the page: *Container8 Asset Management Pty Ltd.* I was ninety-nine per cent positive that this was the company I'd transferred $10,000 to for that US investment back in October.

Even though Amber and I had been exchanging Hamish facts and 'Oh my fucking gods', this development was something I couldn't bring myself to utter out loud. *I couldn't tell her about my money ... I couldn't tell anyone about my money.* It was at this moment that both fear and shame took residence in my body. Thankfully, I didn't have to pretend like things hadn't just become infinitely more stressful because a detective from Manly Police rang, confirmed that Hamish was in custody awaiting a bail hearing, and asked me to come in for questioning as soon as possible.

It's interesting how some people respond to trauma. Instead of asking Amber to drive me to the station, I told her I needed to attend my monthly career coaching session but was going to head to Manly straight after and wanted her to come. Apparently, my initial reaction is a 'trance-like state' followed by 'you need to keep calm and carry on'.

My brain: 'These sessions are expensive and it's too late to cancel without being charged. You can put Hamish aside and talk about your career for one hour.'

Career Coach: 'Hey, Trace! What's been happening with you?'

Me: (bursts into tears) 'I just found out the guy I was dating for a year and a half isn't who he says he was. Apparently, he's a con man who's stolen millions of dollars from people around the world. I … I … I don't know what to say. I don't know what to do. I have to go talk to the detectives I think … I'm so confused.'

Career Coach: 'What the hell are you doing here? Go! We can do this later. Call me if there's anything I can do to help.'

Upon realising that cancelling our session would have been the correct and sensible thing to do, I went back to the office, got Amber and drove to Manly Police station. When we arrived, I was introduced to Tom and Christopher, the lead detectives on what was referred to as Strike Force Garigal. Both young, empathetic and professional, the only information they could give me at that point was that they had arrested Hamish for crimes against three victims and that he was being held at Waverley station in the eastern suburbs. Apparently, they'd released the video of Hamish's arrest and did a Crime Stoppers call-out in the hope that more victims, like myself, would come forward. They knew there was more to uncover. They knew it was big.

It was strange to hear someone refer to me as a 'victim'. Just hours before, it was an identity I never thought I'd have to try on. But as Chris and Tom started interviewing me and I started remembering the different sums of money I'd transferred for Hamish to manage, the title felt more and more fitting. Even though I could easily recall the initial superfund transfer of $187,000, I couldn't recall the exact dates and amounts of the other transactions. Chris and Tom said I would need to map out exactly where, when and how my money got into Hamish's hands as soon as possible. We made a plan for me to come back to the station on 20 July.

As much as I wanted to focus on tracking my money, I couldn't help but be distracted by heartache. My heart was in millions of tiny pieces. The man I knew as Max had been a slow burn, which meant I'd had months to grow close to him; months to learn to trust him, depend on him and ultimately fall in love with him. (As per his plan!) And yet, I now had to fall out of love with him in less than twenty-four hours. With what little information I got about Hamish from Chris and Tom, I realised that on top of finding my money, I would need to help both my mind and heart accept that the man I loved and thought I was going to spend the rest of my life with was fictitious. Max may not have died in a surfing accident as I'd previously feared, but he did in fact die that day. As for Hamish? It became very clear very quickly that he was evil and not to be trusted.

Knowing how hugely devastating this day had been for me, Amber brought me home. Unsure how I was going to keep my composure in front of Asha, I was incredibly grateful when I remembered it was Wednesday … what used to be a glorious kid-free date night with Max. Within hours of me being home, Cath, Pene and another girlfriend, Olivia, came to be by my side. Together, we sat huddled on my lounge in stunned silence watching news clips about Hamish's arrest. There was footage of Lisa Ho, who'd attended Hamish's hearing where he was charged with thirty-one offences and $1.8 million dollars in stolen funds. He'd also had his bail request denied because he was deemed a flight risk. *Who was putting up his bail? Were there still believers?*

The footage that rocked us all the most was of Hamish leaving the courthouse. *How the fuck did this happen?* In our quiet disbelief, we must have looked like a bunch of Gen Z teens because none of us were talking. We were either flicking between news stations or texting each other links to articles we'd found online. At some point, I found myself pushing pulled pork around in a bowl. It was State of Origin night and 'Max' was due to come over for dinner and the footy. That morning before I'd left for work, and before I'd found out Hamish had been arrested, I'd somehow managed to put a pork shoulder into the slow cooker.

I hadn't eaten all day but the ache in my heart was working its way into my stomach. I was nauseated, on edge and hyperaware that my brain was running a million miles a minute trying to piece together the last eighteen months of my life. Every conversation, every look, every text message, email, interaction, person, name, date … Even looking through my rosé-coloured glass of wine, I couldn't see how I was going to come out the other side of this unbroken. Not only was I beginning to grieve a relationship that didn't even exist, I was beginning to realise that I'd most likely lost all the money I'd given Hamish.

'You're handling this really well, Trace,' Olivia said as she cleared the table.

Remember how I said I was once accused of being an emotional desert? It's because I'm not one to scream and cry and roll around on the floor in despair. That doesn't mean I don't feel. I internalise my emotions, which can easily be mistaken as composure. Even my friends couldn't see how rapidly everything was unravelling inside me.

Cath stood up at the table with a cheeky 'Cath grin' and patted my arm. 'Trace, one day, we're going to look back and laugh about this!' she said confidently.

Her comment was just the right amount of comic relief, but as much as I wanted to believe her, I shook my head. 'Too soon, Cath! Too soon.'

CHAPTER 24

Mum/Victim/Sleuth

When I woke up the next morning, it took me a good fifteen seconds to remember why I was being spooned by Cath and wasn't hopping out of bed for my Thursday morning gym session. Oh, that's right – the man I was dating was a criminal and had been arrested. That heart-wrenching, gut-twisting, sinking feeling I'd had the day before immediately returned. Even though I knew I needed to get straight into my forensic accounting tasks for the Manly Police, my first order of action was to protect Asha from the shrapnel that was no doubt coming with Max's exit and Hamish's arrival.

As difficult as it felt, I made the decision to completely shield Asha from everything that was going on. There would be no talk of Max's arrest, no mention of me taking three weeks off work to gather information for the Manly Police and absolutely no tears at the dinner table. This mission was only made possible thanks to Mum, aka Nanny Bootcamp, flying down as soon as she'd heard what had happened. Like me, she couldn't believe that the man who'd pushed her granddaughter onto waves and sat for hours talking Manly NRL footy stars of the 70s was capable of such cruelty. Like always, Mum showed her love by showing up ... and by doing school pick-ups, drop-offs and keeping everyone fed.

My second order of action was tracking down what account my $187,000 cheque had gone into at Bell Potter Securities. The police were particularly keen on this piece of information. It took multiple calls and emails to multiple people at Bell Potter, but I was ultimately told that the cheque had been deposited into a UBIX account owned by Oceania Financial Markets Pty Ltd.

'We don't have any accounts for T Hall Investments Pty Ltd or T Hall Superfund.'

That fucking bastard.

When I pressed for more information, the Bell Potter representative apologised and said it was now a police matter and they couldn't help with anything further.

Seeing as no-one 'official' seemed to want to give me any information, I admit that my own sleuthing may have gotten out of control in these early days. Out of desperation, I continued to message and speak to anyone I could link to Hamish: Sage, the guy from Bondi who Hamish had regularly surfed with; Craig Hall, a life coach I'd met through Hamish and Ana; as well as one of the 'Foster Fam' boys, Matty. The one person I didn't bother contacting was Ana. Why? I wasn't convinced she was another victim of Hamish's. Maybe she had been the one to offer $200,000 in bail? Or the one paying for his lawyers … My ability to trust had been decimated, so why would I put my faith in her to provide me with any answers?

Turns out, Sage had been confused when he'd read the Facebook message I sent him when 'Max' first went missing. Because he'd only known the man in question as 'Hamish', he thought I was referring to another surfing buddy of theirs, Max Menna, who worked at Surfection. I became even more concerned when Max Menna found me on social media and asked why his name was being used in an article about Hamish. After following a link to an article he sent, I learned that someone had incorrectly reported that I knew Hamish as Max Menna. Not only had I never heard of this Max, I also hadn't even spoken to the media at this stage. Max Menna didn't have much helpful information for me; however, he was interested in whether I'd lost money.

Craig Hall was compassionate and told me Hamish had been transferred to Silverwater Correctional Complex. He also told me that Hamish and Ana had only been friends for a few years. She wasn't his boss and they hadn't had a standing twenty-year career together. Ana was an energetics healer. He gave me the phone number I could use to arrange a call with Hamish. *No thanks*.

As for Matty? After days of sleuthing, I finally got his number and sent him a message asking him to take my call. When we finally got on the phone, I was hysterical. He encouraged me to visit Hamish in jail. Not to forgive him but because Hamish wanted to give me information about where my money had gone and how I could get it back.

He pleaded that Hamish had things to tell me that he couldn't say over the phone or in a letter.

'He needs you to know and hear, Tracy,' Matty said.

Fool me once, shame on you. Fool me twice, shame on me. Hamish (and his $317,000 lure) could go fuck himself.

That same day, I got a call from Hamish's niece, Chris and Jules's daughter, who I'd never met. After introducing herself, she explained that Hamish was desperate to talk to me so that he could explain what had happened. He also had a message for me: 'Please tell Tracy to "Just go for a swim in the ocean and wash it all off."'

Go for a swim? Wash it all off? I'm sorry but unless I jumped straight into Fukushima's radioactive water, no amount of scrubbing was going to get the deceit, betrayal and evil off my body. Hamish had lied to me, pretended to love me and then set out to ruin my life. If you're imagining me rhetorically asking his niece, 'Are you for fucking real?' before hanging up in a fit of rage, that's exactly what happened. Remembering you get more bees with honey and that I had yet to connect with Hamish's sister, Jules, I sent his niece a message that night.

Tracy: Thanks for your call today. I am completely numb and just can't believe this has happened. He supposedly loved me and I believed he had my best interests at heart esp being a single mum. I was so fooled. I have so many unanswered questions. I know your mum must be devastated but I would like the opportunity to talk to her either face to face or on the phone. There are just so

many things I don't know the answers to. And I have lost
everything. Just shattered. Thanks. Tracy.

Aside from one text two years later, I never heard from the niece, Chris or Jules again.

My third order of action (when I wasn't sleuthing) was getting to my doctor ASAP. I needed a mental health plan. But probably more importantly, I needed an STD test. I cannot tell you how confronting it is to find out that you don't know the person you're sleeping with. Perhaps the only thing more confronting is finding out that the person who's been loving and cocooning you for the last eighteen months was also plotting to destroy you. I felt financially betrayed and emotionally destroyed and stripped bare of everything I thought was real. *How could he have possibly done this to me?*

Once given the all-clear for venereal diseases and I'd had a solid cry to Bertie with Beth at my feet, I channelled my inner Agatha Christie and got to work figuring out how Hamish had managed to snake his way into my life and metastasise so quickly. Knowing Asha couldn't witness my full-blown investigation, I didn't wallpaper our living room with photos, bank statements, red yarn and push pins so that I could stare at it at 3 am. Instead, my digging was done mostly while sitting hunched at my kitchen bench or over the phone from the alleyway by my house. Every day, I dove deep into text exchanges, the paperwork I'd signed, the accounts I'd opened and the transfers I'd made. I cannot tell you how much it hurts to see it all in one place ...

4 October 2016: $10,000
10 February 2017: $187,000
3 April 2017: $80,000
12 June 2017: $40,000
Total: $317,000

For how much information I managed to gather for the 21-page statement I gave to the police when I went back on 20 July, I couldn't help but feel like I was still missing ninety per cent of the story. My mind mania was out of control, especially late at night. Whether I wanted to or not, I was mentally replaying every conversation, every meeting, every email, every glance, every text message and every handhold; and asking question after question. Surely, it couldn't have *all* been a big fat sham, could it?

Mensa, MIT, Lockheed Martin, the US Treasury ...
was any of that true?
Did he really create Wall Street algorithms?
Did he actually compete in Ironmans?
Was he really engaged to Bec?
Did he live in the same building as Daniel Craig?
Did he even own that $24 million apartment in
New York?
Who took those real estate photos?
Were his parents actually alive?
Had there ever been a foster family?
Why the new alias, Max Tavita?
What name did he book our hotels under?
Were there other women?

Why did he get dressed up for work?
Did he actually go to work in the city?
Did he even work at all?
Was the Singapore work trip made up?
*Is this why he never wanted to fly to Byron Bay
with me?*
What was he really doing on Friday nights?
Why won't Chris and Jules call me back?
Is this why he never wanted me to meet his sister?
*What about the people he did introduce me to? Were
any of them in on his scams?*
What did Ana know?
*Why would Ana go from being a CEO to his
assistant at $200,000 per year?*
How did he pay for all the gifts he gave me?
*Did he own the cars I'd seen? The Porsche, the Aston
Martin, the Range Rovers, the utes ...*
How was this ever going to end well?
Is the tax return he helped me with fraudulent?
Do I have to return my refund?
Was he working alone?
Was he acting under a licence?
*What's going to happen to my self-managed
superfund?*
Who do I report this to?
Who was his accountant?

And then there were the questions I wanted to ask Hamish
directly:

Were you just waiting for my divorce to be finalised?
Were you ever going to tell me?
Was anything you said you felt about me true?
Where is my money?
How do I get it back?

As the weeks ticked by, my shock turned into trauma and betrayal that I felt on every level – intimately, psychologically and financially. The wounds, which were already unlike anything I'd ever experienced, got deeper and deeper every day. Ultimately, I knew that what Hamish had done wasn't the worst thing that had ever happened to me. Prematurely losing Dad and watching Mum battle cancer was far worse. But I'll admit it hit me the hardest because I believed that the whole mess was a reflection of me. It was my choices and my naivety that got me here. Dad dying and Mum getting sick were nothing I could have controlled. But with Hamish – rightly or wrongly – I initially took full responsibility for what happened to me. *How could I have possibly let this happen? Am I really that stupid? Obviously, yes.*

CHAPTER 25

Advice You Can Trust

Every time I looked in the mirror, I saw a 41-year-old woman whose life savings had been obliterated. *I've lost everything.*

Thankfully, the few friends and family members who I'd confided in helped me stay grounded and supported.

'You didn't lose your earning capacity.'

'You didn't lose your daughter.'

'You didn't lose your health.'

'You didn't lose your home.'

'You lost $317,000, not your right to a beautiful life.'

These truths were said with love and sympathy, and were exactly what I needed. But the most significant thing Hamish had robbed me of was my self-confidence. I felt stupid. I felt overwhelmed. I felt like I wasn't capable of rebuilding. Plagued with self-doubt, I knew I needed a professional to help me figure out what moves to make.

The issue was that I didn't trust myself. *What if I make the same mistakes again?*

Even though I had lost faith in my decision-making abilities and felt estranged from my intuition, I went through the motions of what an intelligent person would do in this situation. I asked friends and colleagues for financial advisor recommendations. Next, I checked to make sure they were all licensed, listed on ASIC and didn't have any complaints against them. Finally, I had in-person interviews with my top three picks. My gut told me which one I wanted to hire but my brain urged me to second-guess myself. *Are you sure you're not choosing a dodgy one? Are you sure it's worth paying for financial advice? Maybe you just need to clean up your own mess.*

It took a solid week of convincing myself that I was making the best decision I could with the information I had. (That's the best we can do, right?) I also thought about how I was happy to pay professionals to take care of my car and house repairs, so why wouldn't I pay a professional to help me rebuild my bank accounts? After doing a risk-benefit analysis, I hired a woman named Cathryn. Putting my financial future in someone else's hands again was terrifying, but I knew that playing what few cards I had left in the right way could mean the difference between a life at my desk vs a life after my desk. I also knew that the cost of me not having professional advice was far greater than me having it.

Within weeks of working with Cathryn, I knew I'd made the right decision. She provided me with both hope and a structured plan.

'You will live a great life if you do the things that we agree on,' she said.

These 'things' included making sure I hadn't unknowingly evaded taxes, had an updated will and, most importantly, had a strategic plan to save for my retirement. The bleak reality was that even if I put everything possible into my super from this moment until the end of time, I still wouldn't have enough to live off. At the right time, I would need to consider investing in the stock market and real estate. (Big giant decisions I didn't want to make on my own!)

Once comfortable with choosing my long-term investment strategies, we spoke of ways I could earn and save money in the short term. I went through my budget with a fine-tooth comb, sold a bit of my wardrobe online and said no to trips I would have loved to take with friends and family. I've always thought of money in terms of getting to have experiences, so forgoing travel felt like the biggest sacrifice as I worked to replenish what Hamish had taken from me.

•

My phone rang toward the end of July. Typically, I didn't answer unknown numbers but the newfound sleuth inside me did. *What if it's someone with more information?*

A robotic voice instantly confirmed my worst fear.

'You are about to receive a call from an inmate at Silverwater Correctional Complex. Your conversation will be recorded and may be monitored. The call will last for six minutes. If you do not wish to receive this call, please hang up now.'

The rational part of my brain did not want to accept the call but the part harbouring pain, anger and desperation for answers overpowered it and stayed on the line. I'll tell you this – six minutes may feel long when you're waiting for food to defrost in the office microwave or running on a treadmill but when you're on the phone with your con man ex-boyfriend, it flies! From the moment Hamish said hello, I started hammering him with questions:

'Who are you, REALLY?'

'What is your name?'

'Why did you tell me your name was Max Tavita?'

Thinking he might have a compelling reason such as, 'I was trying to rebuild my life after filing for bankruptcy', or 'I'm a pathological liar', I was stunned when Hamish replied in an off-hand way.

'It's just a name, T! Don't get hung up on a name. It doesn't matter. It's still me.'

Is it?

Next, I asked questions like:

'Are your parents alive?'

'Were you actually engaged?'

My heart was pounding out of my chest the entire time, which made it difficult to hear Hamish's responses. I think he told me that his parents were alive and that he hadn't 'officially' been married because he didn't sign the papers.

Then I asked him:

'What happened to my money?'

'I know there was never a Bell Potter account for T Hall Investments! What account is it in?'

'Is it all in an offshore account in a name that means something to you but can't be traced?'

It's hard to know for sure because I was pacing and rapid-firing questions but I don't remember Hamish being apologetic or helpful. When I realised he wasn't going to tell me anything about my money over the phone, I moved on to questioning the validity of the love and intimacy that we'd shared.

'Was anything you said to me true?'

'Why would you do this? Why?'

I was determined not to let my emotions get the better of me, but by the end of the conversation, I was crying. I admit part of me still wanted to believe that it couldn't have all been fake. Hamish only paused briefly before attempting to reassure me.

'Please trust that I would never hurt you in any way.'

The pure irony of hearing the word 'trust' come out of Hamish's mouth shook me back into reality. This man was never going to give me the answers I was looking for. Strangely, I wanted more than six minutes though. I wanted anyone, including Hamish, to talk to me and tell me the truth. Clearly clutching at straws, I accepted a few more calls from Hamish over the following weeks. Like the first call, I asked questions and Hamish fed me bullshit answers that would temporarily remind me that it was useless seeking any sort of honesty from a con man.

On our final call, Hamish pleaded for me to visit him or at least give him my address so he could write to me.

Simultaneously baffled and relieved by the fact he didn't know my home address, I relented and gave him my work address. *Maybe I'll get answers from his letters.*

Hamish sent five letters between 2 August 2017 and 8 October 2017 and I'll tell you this: no, I did not get answers. For as admirable as his effort was to come across as a decent human, Hamish's words gave me nothing but a multitude of reasons to feel the rage of a thousand fiery suns.

I'm not exaggerating when I say I read Hamish's first letter at least forty or fifty times the week I received it. Even when it wasn't in my hands, I was mentally breaking down every sentence and dissecting every word, all while wondering what reality Hamish could possibly be living in. For example – in the first letter, he wrote:

> I have been stripped of any luxuries, as well as resources
> since I have been here. It took 11 days to get a pen. I am in
> a maximum security facility whilst innocent and have not
> been before a court for trial.

Angered and irritated by his sheer lack of empathy and claims that he was innocent, I nearly keeled over at him saying he had 'no luxuries' in jail and that it took him eleven days to 'get a pen'. He also wrote:

> I didn't ask for any of this, let alone to be torn away from
> our life together [...] Please trust I would never hurt you in
> any way, Tracy.

With no intention of putting actual pen to paper and taking the time to mail anything Hamish could enjoy holding, I mentally drafted numerous responses, including:

Hamish,
You were plotting to steal my life savings and financial independence. You left me with an empty bank account and destroyed every idea I once held about love and humanity. How can that not equate to hurting someone? Sorry it took you eleven days to get a pen. I trust things will get easier for you.
Tracy

Seriously, had Hamish had a frontal lobotomy at Silverwater or was he always this fucked? After placing Hamish's letter in a drawer so I wouldn't compulsively read it anymore, I resumed my part-time job of sleuthing and replenishing my savings. Even though Hamish had stolen $317,000, he hadn't stolen my monthly salary that was still coming in from work or the twenty-plus years I still had to rebuild my finances. Still, it felt like he'd completely levelled me. One would think the police could tell me where Hamish had transferred my funds, but Chris and Tom made it clear I wasn't going to get much information from them, at least not while it was still an 'active investigation'. And as I mentioned before, Bell Potter was remaining very tight-lipped. In hindsight, I wish I'd pushed harder on this and been a squeakier wheel. But honestly, I was so exhausted from trying to find out who Hamish really was and believed that the money trail would be uncovered once he was sentenced. Until then, all I could do was build my own Hamish File.

When I confided in Cath about my need for answers at my place one weekend, she opened up about her own investigation she'd been doing on 'Max' ever since she'd confronted me about him back in March. She'd contacted the National Student Clearinghouse in the US to find any enrolment records for Max Tavita at MIT. *No record.* She'd had a friend who worked in aviation look up historic fatalities involving families. *Nothing.* She also checked the tenancy record at 1 Bligh Street. *No Max Tavita, no Ana Terrén and no family office.* And remember that day I ran into Pene out the front of my house and she gave me $20 for those Lorna Jane leggings? Well, she was actually there because Cath wanted to check the number plates on Max's Mazda ute.

Part of me was upset that Cath hadn't given me the information she was finding out in real time, but we both knew I would have taken her findings straight to Max and that he would have had an answer for everything. Con artists of his calibre always do. Cath also explained that she had been waiting until everything was compiled before confronting me again, so that she'd have the strongest case possible. However, Max was arrested before she got the chance to do so. Cath knew I was seeing Max through oxytocin-coated glasses. She knew that everything and everyone looks different when you're in love.

Recently, I read Abby Ellin's *Duped*. Ellin describes a survey that was conducted on people who'd been warned that they were being deceived. Ninety per cent of 1300 respondents carried on with the relationship or deal anyway. Ellin calls this 'betrayal blindness'. I can tell you that while Hamish's scam became glaringly clear after the fact, I could see nothing but rainbows and moonrises when I was with Max. I admit that when I was confronted by Cath and Kelly, no part of me wanted to accept, believe or even entertain the idea that the guy I was dating wasn't who he said he was. But I'll tell you this – by the time Hamish's second letter arrived, I was seeing his words for exactly what they were. *Utter bullshit.*

> Salt air, your touch, the cocoon, waves breaking, sunshine, coffee. Blue eyes, your smell, your smile, TT, Bub, bronze skin. The ocean, The Mermaid, laughter, hot chips, Coke, terrible singing.

In less than 100 (manic) words, Hamish recapped special moments and inside jokes from our trips to Byron and weekend adventures. His words triggered a slideshow of all the things that led me to what I thought was love, comfort and safety. In reality, he had been leading me straight into his trap. But the most entertaining part?

> I pray that I can see you again soon. Always and forever with love. Xxxxxxxxxxxxxx

Did Australia's biggest atheist find God? The comment that he was praying to see me every day gave me a laugh. As I hadn't done a whole lot of laughing recently, I took that as a tiny win.

I don't want to sound dramatic, but the next two letters made me want to vomit because of how blatantly Hamish was still trying to con me by opening the first letter with:

> Due to not sleeping very much and trying to stay positive, my thoughts drift off to you.

Straight off the bat, he tried to get sympathy by mentioning how hard sleep was to come by and that he struggled to stay positive. Did he not have any clue that in that same period, I could have also written a textbook on insomnia, anxiety and depression?

> I was thinking just now of the time we grabbed the paddleboards and set off from Bronte to Tama for an afternoon jaunt. Your bum was my pillow and your little hands and arms could hardly get any power down though you were trying so hard and never stopped until I told you.

Next, he intentionally listed memories he knew would be emotive and sentimental for me. On the off chance he wasn't trying to lure me back in, was it possible someone could be so misguided and delusional?

> It's like a countdown clock in this place — next second, next minute, next hour, etc. Next legal visit, time outside, meal (of which none are eatable).

This was the only honest thing he wrote — the meals probably weren't 'eatable' because they were too gooey for him.

> I look forward to seeing you, speaking with you soon. I love
> you, Tracy. Forever and always xxxxxxxxxx

As for his requests for me to come to visit? *Hard no.*

It had been less than eight weeks since my world fell apart and I was hanging on by a very thin thread, so I knew better than to waste my scarce time engaging with Hamish. And yet, I just couldn't help drafting mental replies.

> *Dear Hamish,*
> *The idea of visiting you is not scary. I just have*
> *nothing to say to you. I do not believe a word that*
> *comes out of your mouth or precious pen and I have*
> *literally NOTHING to gain from taking time out of*
> *my life to do you a favour by coming and seeing you.*
> *You suspect it will be positive for both of us? What*
> *does that even mean? I'll walk in there, you'll hand*
> *me back my $317,000 and your conscience will be*
> *cleared? Have you considered upping your meds?*
> *Send you photos of us?*
> *Go fuck yourself,*
> *Tracy*

In a moment of weakness (or a tiny last grasp of hope for answers), I ended up writing an actual response and putting it in the mail. Consisting of just two sentences, I sent it partly to find answers and partly to let Hamish know that he'd lost all of my trust.

Hamish,
Give me one good reason I should believe anything you tell
me when everything you've told me over the last 18 months has
been nothing but lies? Why should I trust or believe you after
everything you've done?
Tracy

Okay, so my 'just two sentences' of a letter wasn't as harmless as I thought it would be to send. Hamish sent a huge essay in reply. Within seconds of reading his latest response, I found myself re-reading passages out loud to myself, to Gracie and to Cath before rage-ranting responses I'd never actually send.

The first and simple answer is love.

You don't know what love is … You don't have a
heart or a conscience so how could you?

We fell in love due to shared values, kindness, intimacy and family values.

LIAR! Stealing your girlfriend's life savings isn't
kind. Intimacy? You're borderline asexual. And
family values? I never even met your family. You
wouldn't let me and now I know why. Have you
forgotten that you're estranged from your eldest
sister, pretended your parents were dead and never
introduced me to Jules or her kids?

I can understand how you would have little faith in me.

Can you really though?

I have no photos of you with me but you do. Look at them and I'm sure you've asked yourself was that fake or a dream?

COMPLETELY UTTERLY EMBARRASSINGLY DISGUSTINGLY FAKETY FAKE FAKE FAKE.

Our time together, apart from this chapter, has been amazing.

Our time together IS this chapter. Our entire story is you faking your identity, creating a person you knew I would fall in love with, tricking me into trusting you and then taking EVERYTHING from me. Newsflash … not amazing. Devastating.

I hope in response to your letter I have provided a reason for you to believe and trust in me.

Not even close. You provided no admission of guilt or remorse for taking my money or deceiving me. 'Believe and trust in me?' I can't even find the words to respond to this.

I pray in time we will share and open a new chapter together.

Are you on shrooms?

Sorry for my handwriting, punctuation, spelling. I know how much it annoys you.

Your handwriting and grammar are at the bottom of the list of things I don't respect about you.

If you need to find out about my case or me – contact Murphy's Lawyers.

One of Sydney's top law firms? How are you even paying for this?!

For as cathartic as it felt to spend time figuratively calling bullshit on all of Hamish's words, my brain power and energy for things like work, parenting and rebuilding my life was becoming a limited commodity for obvious reasons. I was running on adrenaline while trying to salvage the dumpster fire Hamish had turned my life into while simultaneously grieving my make-believe relationship with Max. Just because it hadn't been real didn't mean I wasn't still hurting by the loss of the idea of it. Knowing that where attention goes, energy flows and that I did not have any more to spare, I consciously 'cut the cord' to Hamish after that letter and focused on work, Asha and getting support from my inner circle. Work was a particular lifesaver during this time.

On top of providing me with an income, my job was an incredible way to distract myself from the betrayal I felt, the shame I harboured and the fear I had for the future. When I was at work, I was the woman managing teams, agencies and multiple marketing campaigns, not the woman who'd been duped on a dating app. My office became a place of both inspiration and refuge … that is until an unassuming bunch of flowers was delivered to reception in early December. Thinking they were from one of my friends, I excitedly grabbed the vase and walked them to my desk. Fully expecting a sweet note from Cath or thoughtful words from Mum, I opened the card while simultaneously admiring how lovely the native blooms were. In no way shape or form did I expect to read five words that would cause me to sprint to the bathroom to throw up.

SEE YOU SOON. LOVE, HAMISH.

The capitalisation probably wasn't intentional, but whoever wrote the card managed to make Hamish look even more unhinged than he was. I did my best to recentre myself, but thoughts of Hamish 'seeing me soon' had my stalker alarm blaring. Immediately, I called the flower shop to find out who had sent them. Because Hamish couldn't have a credit card in jail, there's no way he could have organised it from the inside. Did this mean he was out of jail? Was he going to be at my house? Or downstairs waiting for me when I finished work? Now I had even more questions I was desperate to find answers to.

Much to my dismay, the florist wouldn't release the information about who the sender was. (A policy that must have been set in place to avoid philandering men being caught by their wives – but becoming a common trend in my search for answers.) Truly rattled, I called

Detective Tom. Tom, dumbfounded and silent at first, reassured me that Hamish wasn't out of jail and that he must have had someone on the outside send the flowers for him. Sensing how upset I was, Tom promised that they were going to take care of it and make sure it didn't happen again. Clearly good at their jobs, this was the last I heard from Hamish.

And to this day, I've never received another letter.

What didn't stop were my tears that I only allowed to surface early in the morning or late at night. For how well I could take a step back and rationalise everything that had happened and was happening, there was no denying just how broken my mind, body and heart were. No matter how much I was told that I was safe, loved, supported and would get back on my feet financially – my mind was telling me otherwise.

CHAPTER 26

What Do You Do Next?

When I was a kid, I used to feel everything so deeply. It didn't matter if I was being rocked by sadness, anger or fear, it was as if I could vividly see the emotion clenching my heart, twisting my stomach or smothering my nose and mouth. Sometimes, it could do all of those things at once. As a way of loosening the grip these emotions would have on me, I would close my eyes and start exploring the corners and curves of each and mentally describe the visceral experience I was having. More often than not, I'd find myself getting lost in the adventure of it all before popping out the other side like a buoy that's been unsuccessfully pushed below the surface. Today, I can see this was a form of meditation. But as a child and young adult, it was simply my way of staying afloat.

By the time Hamish had torn through my life and left me to clean up the aftermath of the death of Max, there was no closing my eyes and exploring the corners and curves of any of the damage he'd caused. The emotions taking hold of my body – which included but were not limited to anguish, despair, rage (as we saw in my imaginary responses to his letters), shame, grief, anxiety and terror – got to live inside me rent-free for a solid three months because I couldn't feel anything other than numb and I was operating on pure adrenaline. Actually, that's not completely accurate. The numbness and adrenaline would lift just enough to allow me to cry every morning and every night.

As much as I would have liked to have been able to have taken more time off work to figure out how I was going to rebuild my bank accounts, self-worth and faith in humanity, I'd exhausted my annual leave. Seeing as I had zero savings (or superannuation) left, there was absolutely no way that I could take my foot off the pedal at work. My cashflow needed to stay consistent, so it didn't matter how sleep-deprived and emotionally numb I felt, I was going to work. Not for me, but for Asha. She was the only hope I had left. Here's an uncomfortable truth: if I hadn't had the role of 'Mum' to play, I'm pretty sure I would have stayed in bed and rotted in my own skin. Depression was grabbing hold of me but I was determined not to let it swallow me whole. I couldn't. I had school lunches to make and class projects to help with.

In those first few months of adjusting to a post-Max world, I did all the things one who is reeling from a traumatic experience does to cope. First, I drank alcohol every night. The first drink made me feel soothed. The second one brought me back to my desired numb state.

The third and sometimes fourth? Well, those just made everything worse. Next, anxiety robbed me of my desire and ability to eat, and I lost six kilos in three weeks. My stomach was in perpetual knots and I couldn't hold onto any food – from either end. And finally, I intentionally made my life very small; partly to avoid the embarrassment of people knowing what had happened and partly because I didn't have energy for pretty much anyone or anything. The thought of having to turn up to an event, birthday or work function filled me with instant dread. Aside from my family, I really only caught up with my close girlfriends and my long-time friend Tim.

Tim and I had met some fifteen years earlier when we worked together at that start-up hedge fund. When our careers took us in different directions, we kept in touch here and there, but it wasn't until I ran into him in late 2016 when I was dating Max that we reconnected. He was in the throes of a divorce, which made us great sounding boards and support systems for each other. Because Max was pretty anti-social and typically unavailable on a Friday night, Tim and I quickly became tried and trusted plus-one dates when needed. We had that long-term friend familiarity that made hanging out so incredibly easy and fun.

During one of our 'clearly we need to get Tracy out of the house' beach walks, Tim and I sat by the water after grabbing a coffee. Hard to ignore the abundance of happy couples and families around us, Tim asked, 'Do you think you'll ever be able to love again?'

I didn't mean for them to but tears suddenly streamed down my face. The sinking feeling I'd learned to live with felt even heavier. All I could do was mutter, 'I don't know.' Because I actually didn't. How could I ever trust another man again?

When I wasn't working, mothering, sleuthing, walking with friends like Tim or lying in bed feeling heavy and full of despair, I was mostly thinking about how much I hated feeling like this. Upon recognising that alcohol and avoiding food was not helpful, I cut my alcohol intake and prioritised eating frequent small meals. Yes, I still needed ways to cope, but they needed to be sustainable. At therapy, I was reminded that I should prioritise exercising, sleeping and keeping a gratitude journal.

Movement and exercise have always been life for me, so that was the first thing I tried to find a way to make happen daily. Aside from Thursday mornings and every other weekend, I couldn't see where I could fit it in. When expressing these limiting beliefs to a well-meaning friend, she gave me possibly the worst advice someone in a freshly traumatised state should receive. She suggested the solution was for me to pay for a babysitter to come at 5.30 am so I could go for a run at 6 am before work. Hoping the endorphins would cure me (and honestly happy to try anything at this point to make me feel better), I scraped money together for the sitter, dragged my sleep-deprived body out of bed and attempted to run to Shelly Beach and back. Ten minutes in, I found myself walking along the beachfront at Manly, bawling my eyes out. Everything hurt. My lungs, my muscles, my mind, my heart, my feet. I was exhausted. With tears streaming down my face, I sat on one of the benches overlooking the ocean as waves beat down on the shore, and wished in that moment that I was being tossed around in the whitewash so those waves could swallow me up whole.

Seeing as I was only averaging four hours of sleep a night, the last thing I should have done was forgo the potential of getting more sleep only to deplete myself further. This was a pretty messed-up moment for me, which is why I only did it once. Truthfully, the best thing I could do for my body was yin yoga, easy walks and prioritising rest. Much to my surprise, the gratitude journal proved to be one of the best ways of helping me believe that the world wasn't completely fucked. Some days, I would write that I was grateful for the sunrise, Mum's voice or Asha's hugs. Other days it felt like I was scraping the bottom of the barrel …

Today, I'm grateful for: An uneventful bus ride. (I got a seat and no-one smelled like urine.)

Today, I'm grateful for: My Woolies delivery turning up on time.

Today, I'm grateful for: Hot chips and chicken salt.

When my therapist and I realised I'd hit the three-month mark post-con man, she was surprised to hear that I was still crying every night and most mornings, felt like I was operating with a heavy grey blanket over me and dreaded most interactions so was isolating myself more and more. She also didn't love that I wanted to just 'run away' and 'disappear'.

'Is that not normal?' I asked genuinely.

'I'm concerned. Look, you have very valid reasons to cry every day, but this isn't sustainable. You might want to consider talking to your GP about taking an antidepressant or anxiety medication. It's okay to get additional help.'

For no other reason than thinking I should be able to handle such a life blow, I admit that I was resistant at first. But after yet another morning of muffling sobs with my pillow so Asha couldn't hear, I decided to give it a go. A close friend had told me I might feel worse before I felt better, but I was truly surprised by just how rocky weaning onto medication was. For weeks, I walked around feeling like my world had been muted. Then there was a period where I felt even more anxious and on edge. But then one evening about a month later, I was crawling into bed feeling unfamiliarly calm. As I pulled my doona up and tucked it around my body, I had the most soothing thought – *I haven't cried today.* Even more soothing – *I don't feel like crying now either!* The medication was working. From that moment, I began to feel more and more hopeful in every sense of the word. *Maybe I can get through this?*

When Dad died, I remember thinking that it was incredibly self-indulgent to sit and ponder, wonder and deeply examine something that I had no way of ever changing the outcome of. Surely it was more productive, more worthy or simply more sensible to just get on with it. *Suck it up, princess, you'll be right.* But suck it up, I did. As you recall, I sucked it up so hard I ended up choking and ran away to India. With the aid of my antidepressants, I was finally clear-headed enough to see that even though it was complicated and multi-layered, I needed to mourn the loss of Max and my financial future. This time, I decided not to do the same 'nothingness' as I did with my dad. Instead, I was going to do two things: grieve wholeheartedly and let myself be easily pleased. Anytime I was out, I started noticing small things, like someone letting me in when I was in traffic or the smile on a kid's face as they patted a dog. Over time, these micro moments of happiness added up and started to condition me to look for wonder as I waded my way through grief.

●

When you experience death, betrayal, trauma or any event that makes you feel off-kilter, it's inevitable that you or someone else will comment, 'There's a reason for everything.' (PSA: Please don't say this.) Next, you'll be prompted to answer questions such as, 'What can you learn from this?', 'How can you grow?', 'What's the most helpful way to move forward?' Personally, I don't always think there's a reason for everything. Bad things happen to good people and good things happen to bad people and that's that. However, I do think the universe has a way of nudging us to reach our full potential and purpose, which is why so much of my grieving process involved me trying to figure out what I could learn from my time with Hamish McLaren. Much of this introspection was done bobbing in the ocean on my surfboard between waves or late at night in my journal. Perhaps some of the most eye-opening work was done during my week-long stay at a health retreat in the Gold Coast hinterland in early 2018.

You're probably thinking, *Girl – you just lost $317,000. How are you fitting a week-long stay at a health retreat into your budget?!* Don't worry – I had that thought too. But like investing in a financial advisor, I wanted to invest in my healing, and knew I needed to get the biggest impact in the shortest amount of time. I thought about having a staycation but I didn't want to be alone and I didn't want to be at home without Asha. Even today, I don't like being at home when she isn't there for more than a few days. It just feels empty and quiet. By living well below my means, I was able to head somewhere that would allow me to heal, be fed, rest and try to recentre. I wasn't going to kick back and read a Liane Moriarty novel. I was going to do the deep work needed to release the attachments I'd formed, reframe the unhelpful narratives I was writing and uncover the fears that were driving my actions. But if I could squeeze in a sneaky massage and nap by the pool to pay down my sleep debt, you bet your bottom dollar I was going to lap that right up.

Depending on the health retreat, the entire experience can feel a lot like adult summer camp. As a single parent who has decision-making fatigue, I loved the idea of someone telling me what to eat, where to be and when to go to sleep. At this particular one, there were set times for meals, daily optional activities and the type of bonding you can only do when you think you're never going to see someone again. Throughout my stay, I shared bits and pieces of my story when it felt safe, but mostly I kept to myself and focused on detaching from the future I thought I was going to have with Max ... as well as the financial security Future Me had been banking on. Perhaps the most profound experience I had came halfway through my stay when I signed up for equine therapy.

Have you seen the movie *28 Days*? It's the one where Sandra Bullock is an alcoholic staying at a 28-day treatment facility. I found myself in a situation not too dissimilar to the iconic scene where Sandra is trying to get a horse to let her lift its hoof. Only difference, I was trying to hold my ground telepathically/energetically between two horses who were getting very much up in my personal space. I thought I was doing a great job when the woman leading the session swiftly and unexpectedly moved in to block me from being bitten. *Maybe I'm not as good at this as I thought.*

'Did you not see Mocha try to bite you? He was pushing you out of your space and was about to bite your ear and you had absolutely no idea. What do you think this could mean for you?'

What a question. No, I had not seen Mocha try to bite me. I suddenly burst into tears, thinking about the relevance of this situation and wondered what it could mean. *Am I too trusting? Am I incapable of sensing danger? Is this how I missed the truth about Max? He was in my space about to bite me and I had no idea. What an idiot I was and what an idiot I still am.*

Those questions somehow saw me spiral into a complete existential crisis. How could I ever trust anyone again when I couldn't even trust myself to notice when I'm in danger? Up until Max Tavita became Hamish McLaren in 2017, I truly believed that ninety-nine per cent of people were inherently good and could be trusted. I also believed that I had a strong intuition, was a great judge of character and was going to spend the next forty-something years of my life with someone who saw and supported me on every level and in every life area.

Looking back on my life before Hamish, my willingness to trust my parents, siblings, friends, teachers, colleagues, romantic partners, airline pilots, fellow drivers on the road, doctors, bankers and hairdressers had served me well. Of course, there were missteps, misfortunes and momentary lapses in judgement that led to emotional and physical bruising, but for the most part, I could always use hope and optimism to pick myself up and keep moving forward.

However, the hope I once easily tapped into was now nowhere near as strong as my crippling self-doubt. I no longer had faith in my own ability to judge and trust someone. Should I have had a stronger intuition about who Max really was and what he was after? Should I have been more suspicious? Was I blind to all the red flags? Was I to blame for all this?

By the time I was leaving the health retreat, I still wasn't sure about the answers to these questions. It was clear that it was going to take much longer than seven days of biodynamic meals and colonics to figure out what I was going to learn from Hamish McLaren. However, I knew I was making steps in the right direction – it was just going to take time.

●

While catching up with Cath after my retreat, she suggested that I connect with her good friend and investigative journalist for *The Australian*, Greg Bearup. They'd spoken about what had happened to me and Greg was interested in writing a story about Hamish. While I could see the benefits of working with a journalist due to the level of access to court records they're typically granted, as well as shining a light on who Hamish really was, I knew I wasn't ready for any level of potential publicity. In fact, I was not ready, full stop. To be honest, there were quite a few things I wasn't ready for.

For starters, I still really didn't want people outside of my trusted inner circle to know about the money I had lost and the depths of the deceit. On top of a sense of shame and embarrassment, there was the fear of it being used against me. There was also so much uncertainty around whether I'd get my money back or not. Some people made me feel hopeful, while others had a much more dire outlook on the situation. Either way, I didn't want to talk about it until I knew what was going to happen. Hamish's plea hearing date had been pushed back numerous times, which was leaving me frustrated and mentally drained.

The months ticked by and I still didn't know how Hamish was going to plead. All I could really do was continue to work, journal, go to therapy, practise yoga, work my way up from walking to running and have conversations with best friends that left me feeling nourished and empowered. Perhaps the most important thing I did was sit with it. 'It' being the heartache, angst, regret, fear and sadness Hamish had stirred up inside me. They say time heals all wounds and I concur … that is, *if* you're using your time to go within, do the work, rest, heal and consciously decide how you want to respond to the events in your life.

One morning shortly after the one-year anniversary of Hamish's arrest, I woke up with the strongest intense inner 'knowing' – that it was going to take someone a whole lot more impressive than Hamish to break me and keep me down. This wasn't some conceited internal cheer or pep talk I was giving myself, nor was it a repetitive motivational quote or manifestation chant. It was something I genuinely felt inside my heart and my head, and it helped me realise what I needed to do with all my grief, anger, hurt, shame, tears, embarrassment and ever-growing list of questions. I was going to call Greg Bearup from *The Australian* and tell him that I was ready to talk. It was time to get answers, it was time to shine a light on intimate fraud and it was certainly time to do whatever was necessary to make sure Hamish didn't get the chance to strike again.

CHAPTER 27

Nobody Likes an Unfinished Story

Around the time I matched with Max Tavita on Happn, the Russian–American author Maria Konnikova was celebrating the release of her book *The Confidence Game: Why We Fall For It … Every Time*. Fortunately for Hamish, I didn't get my hands on a copy of her book until after he'd done his dirty work. If I had, I dare say I'd be writing this chapter $317,000 richer. Insightful and easy to read, I don't think I've ever felt more 'seen' by a book. Given that the pages of my copy are highlighted and marked with sticky notes, I have to really hold back from not regurgitating all the brilliance delivered in each chapter. (Seriously, go read it!) But one thing I must draw attention to is the part where Maria points out that our minds are built for stories and that humans don't like to exist in a state of uncertainty or ambiguity. When stories aren't readily available, we create them.

And when stories aren't finished, it makes sense that we won't want to rest until we find the missing pieces.

When Cath teed up an initial lunch meeting to introduce me to Greg Bearup in early August 2018, I really didn't know what our talk would amount to. All I knew was that there was more to uncover, more to expose and more for people to learn from. Greg, an award-winning journalist and author renowned for his investigations in Australia and abroad, was a trusted friend of Cath and Brendan's and someone I was keen on helping me figure out the rest of my story. Over lunch, we spoke briefly of my relationship with Max and how Cath had had her spidey senses on full alert from nearly day dot.

Cath explained, 'For starters, his name was Max Tavita. "Tavita" is a Cook Islander name and Max looks like a fucking albino!'

Greg had seen Cath's dossier on Max. He commented that it's much easier for someone who's not in the relationship to see red flags. Many people have written and spoken about con artists really just being a magician or illusionist. When you're sitting in the front row like I was, all you can see is the magic. But when you're in the wings, like Cath, that's when you can spot the tricks. Like me, Greg was eager to find out the full extent of Hamish's tricks and shared that he wanted to write an investigative piece on him.

For as much as I wanted to start a much-needed conversation around intimate fraud and con artists in general, I didn't want to be involved if it was going to be a series of click-bait headlines like 'Naive and Vulnerable:

Meet All the Women Who Swiped Right on Mr Wrong'. Greg, who admittedly didn't know what the story was going to be yet, assured me that, regardless, it would definitely not be written that way because he presents facts and the fact was: I wasn't a naive woman. Once in agreement, we made a plan to meet again for him to interview me.

Greg and I had our second meeting at a cafe across from his Newscorp office in Surry Hills. I quickly learned that he was calm, kind, funny, incredibly smart and, above all, empathetic. Greg focused on getting a clear picture of how Hamish had worked his way into my life as 'Max' and was curious about his personality, mannerisms and manipulation tactics. Midway through the interview, he decided that it would be helpful if we went across the street to his office so he could record what I was saying. Once mic'd up, I continued telling him about the 'Tracy and Max' saga and also gave him information on the case from my discussions with police.

'Fuck, what a story,' Greg said after switching off my mic.

A story, indeed. By this point in time, I'd already delivered my 'story' to police, accountants, the ATO, lawyers, my bosses, therapists, friends and to myself on multiple occasions. It didn't seem to matter how many times I told it, I was always left with more questions than answers because the more questions people asked me, the more I realised just how much I didn't know about the man I'd given my love, trust and money.

'If only I wasn't the main character,' I said.

Before I left, we talked about Hamish's plea hearing, which was finally taking place on 5 September at the Sydney

Central Local Court. Greg offered to come with me, which I happily accepted. For the last twelve months, I had been dreading the day I would cross paths with Hamish. At first, there was the fear of him being released. After the flowers arrived, there was the fear of him showing up outside my office or – worse – knocking on my door. Thankfully, our encounter was going to be with him handcuffed and wearing a green jumpsuit in a glass box surrounded by two large guards.

On the morning of the plea hearing, I took extra care to make sure my outfit (white jeans, denim top and loafers) and hair were on point because I wanted to feel my absolute best. To be clear – I didn't care how I looked to Hamish. It was more about my own confidence at this point. Feeling strong, I walked into Sydney Central Local Court with Greg, Cath and Emily by my side. Arguably the most important accessories I could have chosen that day, Cath and Emily were serving up major 'don't fuck with our girl' vibes while I was doing my best to channel 'stoic and unbreakable'.

While feeding our items through an x-ray machine and walking through the metal detector, I took note of how dated and musty the building was. Emily commented that it felt eerie and cold. After collecting our items, Greg led us to a noticeboard that listed what room to go to. I was grateful that Greg knew what to do. Fully expecting the room to be packed with conflicted family members, angry victims and rows of hungry-for-the-money-shot photographers and journalists, I think we were all a bit surprised to learn that aside from the judge, the DPP (director of public prosecutions), Hamish's legal aid and two prison guards, we four were pretty much the only people who seemed to care what happened to Hamish McLaren.

As the judge was taking their seat and shuffling a few papers around, I pondered that surely there must be other people who wanted to see Hamish held accountable or at the very least some of his family members. In the lead-up to the hearing, Detective Tom had been keeping me in the loop of Hamish's case, such as if there'd been new developments or we were expecting more delays. I was surprised not to see him there. Before I could think too much about it, my eyes caught sight of Hamish's blindingly blond hair and bald patch making its way up from an underground staircase.

Instantly, my heart started racing, breathing became difficult and every part of my body was flooded with heat. Feeling sick to my stomach, I clenched my jaw as a precautionary measure and then broke into a sweat. Even though the rational part of my brain knew I wasn't in danger anymore (mostly because of the built-like-a-brick-shit-house guards on either side of Hamish), my body clearly did not get the memo. *The body really does keep the score.*

In the years following this day, I would go on to do countless hours of EMDR (eye movement desensitisation and reprocessing) therapy and somatic work to remove the physical memory of Hamish and my body's automatic defence response that seemed to happen on a cellular level. But well before I was reprogramming my brain and body, I was just a girl (looking really classy and cute in chambray) sitting in front of a boy (in an ill-fitting green jumpsuit), hoping he'd plead guilty.

Due to where we were sitting, I could really only see the profile of Hamish's face; one that wore a cold and vacant expression. Even with my partial view, I could tell that Hamish was finally looking like his true self. After listening to a few formalities and legal jargon I only know from reruns of *Ally McBeal*, the judge began to read out the charges. Hamish looked dead straight ahead as he pleaded guilty to seventeen counts of dishonestly obtaining financial advantage by deception and one count of knowingly dealing with proceeds of crime. Not once did he glance around to see who was in the room. To this day I still wonder *why* he didn't look to see if I was there. Was it remorse? I like to think he felt so bad he couldn't look me in the eye. Or maybe he was the emotional desert and was dead inside. If I had to put money on it, I'd bet that he was simply adopting his next identity: obedient inmate who deserves a second chance.

Within minutes, Hamish was taken back down the staircase and we were left to absorb what his guilty plea meant. *No trial!* Cath, Emily and I squeezed hands and felt relieved that Hamish was going straight back to jail. For how long? That we still didn't know. Greg momentarily stopped writing notes to share in my relief that I wouldn't have to testify. There were hugs, a few tears and a whole lot of work to do. This was really just the beginning.

Before we left the room, the DPP came over and introduced himself. Upon learning that I was one of the victims, he offered (what seemed to be) genuine condolences. Throughout the plea hearing, I kept hearing discussions about the Statement of Facts document. Curious as to what it contained, I asked the DPP if I could have a copy of the Statement of Facts so I could better understand what he, the judge and Hamish's defence were referring to in the session. For reasons I still don't know, I was told no. Just when I thought I'd hit another dead end, Greg waved his journalist badge and was suddenly given a still-warm-from-the-photocopy-machine stack of papers. (Hot tip: if you need information regarding a case you're involved in, talk to a journalist or get the media involved.)

Greg, Em, Cath and I went straight to a cafe, divided the paper into four piles and began poring over the pages. Just like when I'd been on a Google mission with Amber on the day Hamish was arrested, we had a rapid-fire exchange of 'Hamish facts'. Turns out that instead of just three other victims and $1.8 million in missing money which the police had mentioned to me when I gave my statement a year before, there were now fifteen victims in Australia pressing charges for losses totalling $7.66 million.

Greg looked up from his stack of papers and said, 'This story is huge. This is a podcast.'

As a self-confessed podcast junkie (e.g. you had me at *Serial*), I had a pretty good idea of just how impactful a podcast can be. But was I ready for the world to know that I was Hamish McLaren's last victim? My gut was telling me yes but, as you'll recall, the only thing Hamish didn't take from me was self-doubt. In fact, he amplified it on his way out.

Over the next few weeks, I spoke to close friends and family members about the idea of being involved in an investigative podcast. For the most part, they were quite positive. But some were adamant that it would ruin my career and reputation to speak so openly about 'being duped'. I could tell these people were coming from a place of love and wanted to protect me, but my gut wasn't having it. A strong voice inside of me kept saying, *This is the whole problem. This is why it is still happening. No-one wants to talk about intimate fraud. No-one wants to talk about money. And if no-one is talking about it, how are we ever going to stop it from happening?*

Mostly, it was important for me to know that Greg and I agreed on what our objectives were. Ultimately, my goal of coming forward and speaking publicly about what happened was to: a) uncover the truth of who Hamish really is; b) help prevent others from falling prey to intimate fraud; and c) get the answers for anyone who's been harmed by Hamish. Upon completing a thorough and peer-reviewed pros and cons list, I shook hands with my gut and said we had a deal. I was doing the podcast. So what if people thought less of me? Conversations around fraud, vulnerability and the true price of trust need to be had. I knew who I was and if someone was going to judge me or think less of me because of this, I was happy for them to not be in my life.

Coming Out of the Dark

From the word *go*, Greg began following leads, interviewing the other known victims and tracking down old connections. Almost daily, I'd get emails, calls or texts from Greg with updates like, 'I just spoke to Hamish's ex-wife!'

The ex-wife Greg was referring to is Bec Rosen. Although still a victim of Hamish in many aspects, Bec wasn't cited in my case because she didn't technically lose any money. As you may recall, Hamish told me that he had been engaged to Bec and that she was an alcoholic. When Greg spoke to Bec, he learned that Hamish had been married to Bec, who is certainly not an alcoholic. After Greg got her permission to pass her number to me, I reached out to Bec within a few days. We shared our experiences with Hamish and very soon became close friends.

As I listened to Bec describe the reality of her relationship with Hamish, it became clear that Hamish seemed to follow a 2:1 Rule. Meaning, his stories were either made up of two truths and one lie or two lies and one truth. For example, he and Bec were engaged (before they were married) and they did attend couples therapy in Glebe. Now, here's where it gets really twisted. Their relationship didn't break down due to her alleged alcoholism. It broke down because Hamish had an affair with her son's teenage girlfriend, who asked to be identified as Jane. Hamish convinced Jane's grandparents, Peter and Lorraine Cross – victims cited in my case – to invest their entire retirement fund, $1.7 million, in his dodgy superannuation scheme. They recouped $569,196. $1,143,304 remains missing.

Bec, Jane, Peter and Lorraine were just the tip of the iceberg. Greg, who always seemed to be in a perpetual state of disbelief and often started his correspondence with lines like, 'Trace, cop a load of this!' or 'You're not going to believe what I just found!', gave me a rundown on the other victims in my case.

In addition to myself and Peter and Lorraine Cross, there were:

- Lisa Ho, an Australian fashion designer who trusted Hamish to invest $850,000 of her superannuation money. She recouped $500,000. Lisa, the powerhouse she is, was actually responsible for Hamish's bankruptcy in 2016. Sadly, no authorities seemed to notice the company he ran under his sister Jules's name, Oceania Financial Markets.

- Glenn and Vickie Pickard, a Mudgee couple who lost $607,600 out of the $754,900 they entrusted Hamish to invest.
- Karen Lowe, a Mosman woman who Hamish convinced to take out a $1.3 million dollar loan, lost $950,000. (Karen is also the woman who Max was speaking terribly about at Fu Manchu when I wanted to disappear into my dumplings.)
- A Sydney woman who trusted Hamish to invest her divorce settlement and family inheritance totalling $564,696.66. She was only able to recoup $237,900.
- One of Hamish's fellow triathletes lost $428,000 out of the $515,000 he entrusted Hamish to manage in the self-managed superfund he'd 'set up' for him.
- A woman introduced to Hamish via Ana Terrén lost $768,847.74 of the $820,647.74 she believed Hamish was investing for her.
- Two co-owners of a surf shop lost $33,270.42 after Hamish inserted himself in a private legal negotiation.
- A woman lost $1,019,000 of the $1,049,000 that Hamish said he was investing across two funds.
- Another woman introduced to Hamish via Ana Terrén lost $80,400 of the $100,000 she entrusted Hamish to invest.

When I became one of Hamish's victims, I was forced to join a club that nobody wants to be part of. The only positive thing the Hamish Club offered was the chance to meet people who knew exactly what it was like to have your past and future stolen from you. Just as I bonded with Bec, I'd go on to become close with Karen Lowe and Jane.

By stealing my superannuation and the money from the shares I'd earned, Hamish effectively stole a portion of every hour that I had worked in my career. Even though that was difficult to accept, I and many of my fellow club members knew that we still had a future. We would and will rebuild. Others weren't so lucky because they didn't have time on their side to recoup any losses. My heart felt deeply sad for them. But there was one member of the club who had a different story: Jane. She had been the girlfriend of Bec's teenage son.

Before Hamish's parasitic impact on her life, Jane was known to be an extremely intelligent, athletic, kind and happy teen who'd overcome a rocky home life. But then Hamish came along. He groomed her into having an affair with him, all in a bid to swindle her grandparents out of an enormous amount of money. While she didn't experience the financial devastation directly, Hamish left her feeling violated, mortified, remorseful, ashamed and burdened with an overwhelming amount of guilt. Try finishing Year 12 with that on your plate.

Even just a month into Greg's investigation, I was highly aware of how healing the entire process was for me. Exciting, cathartic, shocking, comforting, exposing, sometimes confusing, but mostly very healing. I loved getting answers, I loved meeting women like Bec and Karen, and I loved that I was finally and fully understanding who the hell Hamish was. Jane, understandably, was hesitant to speak with Greg at first, but I like to think it helped her see that she is an incredibly intelligent, kind and talented woman who deserves to feel stronger from her experience, not weaker. Thankfully, Jane was able to repair her relationship with both Bec and her son and, like me, has since gone on to garner invaluable support from other victims.

While I was healing and developing these friendships, Greg was gathering evidence that indicated Hamish's damage spanned much further than fifteen victims. In fact, it looked like it spanned across three decades and multiple countries including Australia, the US, the UK, Canada and Hong Kong. By the time Greg had completed his nearly year-long investigation and the podcast was in post-production, we had reason to believe that Hamish had likely stolen far more than $7.66 million. In fact, it's probably closer to $80 million, if not $100 million. So why didn't more people come forward? One theory is that many of Hamish's victims are men, some of whom admitted to Greg that they are too proud and/or ashamed to say they were conned. Others said they were so done with the trauma that they wanted to leave it in the past. I can see why they'd want to stay silent. However, I can also see just how dangerous it is to do so. For me, at least.

American professor and author Brené Brown wrote in *Daring Greatly* that 'Shame is the fear of disconnection... the intensely painful feeling or experience of believing that we are flawed and therefore unworthy of love and belonging.' If there's one thing I've learned from being a member of the Hamish Club, it's that shame seems to thrive in the dark. Until I started talking about what happened, the shame I felt about falling victim to a white-collar crime festered until it threatened my relationships with friends, potential partners and, ultimately, myself. By shining light on my story, I hoped to not only rebuild my connections, but also be brave enough to stay open for new ones.

Luckily for me, when *Who the Hell is Hamish?* landed in podcast apps in February 2019, phone calls, texts and DMs from friends (old and new), acquaintances, colleagues and strangers came flooding in. While many were commending me for my bravery and strength, I was shocked by how many people wanted to share their own stories of being the victim of intimate fraud or an investment scam. One woman in particular has always stuck with me. When her marriage ended in her late thirties, she trusted a 'friend' to invest her divorce settlement and lost the whole thing. Now in her seventies, she had never told a soul, not even her children, until reaching out to me.

I can't imagine how hard it would have been to carry that around for so long and I hope that woman experienced the relief I'd felt when I began to truly understand that cons can happen to anyone. It doesn't matter your gender, age, education or any of your other qualities; if you're human, you are susceptible. Knowing how powerful and healing sharing stories can be, I encouraged any and all conversations with anyone who'd experienced financial deception or intimate fraud, which, in a way, helped me unpack my own. These stories were so different to the ones I'd heard on the likes of tabloid television shows like *A Current Affair*. I could never relate to these stories. But the ones that landed in my DMs and inbox were as deep, complex and as calculated as my own. I was 100 per cent there for that.

As I read messages from people in the US, Europe, South America, Sweden and beyond, I learned that I wasn't just a member of the Hamish Club; I was also a member of the ever-growing club of global romance scam victims. We don't have an official name but I'm thinking it should be called the Victims of Irreverent Psychopaths (VIP) Club. Here's what's hard about being a VIP Club member: anyone who's not in the club probably doesn't *really* understand how something like this could happen. The truth is, most people think what happened to me would never happen to them. I have no doubt that it's easy for some people to sit here and read my story while proudly pointing out every beige, pink and red flag.

Here's the thing – court cases in general have a way of making intimate fraud and investment scams look very factual when, in reality, they are every bit as complicated as that relationship you had in your twenties. On the flip side, the media sensationalises elements of the story. Criminals like Hamish don't just 'pull a fast one'. They meticulously work their way into the fabric of your very being, infiltrate or draw you away from your social life and then leverage your emotions over a long period of time to extract money. Yes, the financial loss can feel catastrophic, but money is money and there's more of that if you work hard and put a plan in place. Plus, people lose money from genuine investments all the time. What truly bonds VIP Club members is the emotional betrayal. It's one thing to rebuild your bank account. It's quite another to rebuild your soul and faith in humanity.

What's wonderful about being a VIP Club member is that I've met many more people just like Bec, Karen and

Jane ... People who listen with extreme empathy, pass zero judgement and know that just because something is over doesn't mean you're ever going to be 'over it'. As someone who prided herself on her resilience and strength, I cannot tell you how disappointing it was to realise that 'moving on' was going to take much longer than two years and a podcast. When *Who the Hell is Hamish?* was released, Hamish had yet to be sentenced and I, like many of his other victims, was still actively working on how to exist with the shame, guilt and fear that he had left in his wake.

Of course, every puzzle piece that was uncovered through Greg's investigation gave us each some sort of 'peace' but I think we were (and are) pretty realistic that Hamish McLaren was never going to be a past experience. The lifelong healing we have to actively do makes him a living experience that we most likely won't 'move on' from. Instead, he's an experience we must continually move through, move with. Some days, it feels like a breeze; other days, it's really tough. To be fair, his sentencing did give us a glimpse at that elusive 'closure' so many speak of. That particular door would be shut. But this is a big house with many doors and rooms to discover and organise in my brain.

•

In the weeks leading up to the 20 June 2019 sentencing date, my sleep was awful. The hearing had been delayed by months on multiple occasions, and I was feeling increasingly anxious. The first major delay happened in

February, when Hamish's barrister said that a psychologist and psychiatrist had discovered that Hamish may have a mental health condition and that he might not be fit to stand trial. When the judge pressed for more information, the barrister elaborated that it may have to do with autism. (My eyeroll was audible when I found this out ... wasn't this just another fabrication?) In order to proceed with the hearing, Hamish ended up being evaluated by court-approved doctors and was not found to have autism but to be someone 'with a long-standing pattern of inherent maladaptive personality traits and who uses dishonesty and manipulation for personal gain'. Now that, I believed.

When a text came through the day before confirming it was all systems go, I didn't know what to do with myself. Should I sit, stand, pace or curl up in the foetal position? After two long years of wondering what Hamish McLaren's fate was, we were all finally going to get the answer. I ended up spending a bit of time doing all of the things – sitting, standing, pacing and, literally, curling up in the foetal position, before realising exactly what I wanted to do ... I wanted to do something symbolic. Something that Hamish couldn't.

Instantly, I sprang up from my living room floor, threw on swimmers, shorts and laced up my running shoes. As soon as I was out the front door of my building, my feet pounded the pavement and did not stop until I'd run to Shelly Beach and back. Hot, sweaty, full of endorphins and absolutely delighted by the warmth of the winter sun on my skin, I made my way down the path onto Freshwater Beach. After dropping my stuff in a pile, I took a deep breath before running straight into the water and letting the waves wash it all away.

Okay, so I knew this ocean bath wasn't going to 'wash it all away'. But I did know it felt like a nice big FUCK YOU to Hamish, a man who loved nothing more than running and ocean swims. In between floating on my back and tasting the saltwater between my lips, I let the gratitude for my freedom and Mother Earth wash over me. On my walk back to my house, I pictured Hamish exactly where he deserved to be: in his ugly green prison clothes, locked up and away from all that's beautiful in the world.

CHAPTER 29

Justice

On the morning of the sentencing, Greg met me in Freshwater and we took a cab to Downing Centre Local & District Court on Liverpool Street to see the man who invented Max Tavita be given his sentence. Greg, who was holding a microphone between us, interviewed me about how I was feeling. Honestly, I felt excited for it to happen and ready for it to be over at the same time. I, like so many others, wanted to know where Hamish was going to be for the next period of time and for how long. I thought 'life' would be good but it probably wasn't reasonable or realistic.

On one hand, I wanted Hamish to get life because he had stolen everything I had at the time. On the other hand, I wanted him to get life because I have zero doubt that if given the chance, he will absolutely reoffend. Considering how difficult it had been to bring charges against Hamish at all, as well as how lenient the court can sometimes be on this type of crime, I didn't want to get my hopes up too much. In an effort to understand the Australian legal system, I turned to Google and read that judges look at five factors when determining the seriousness of white-collar fraud.

1. The amount of money
2. The length of time over which the offending took place
3. The motive for the crime
4. The level of planning and sophistication
5. The breach of trust

While wearing a metaphorical bench wig, I thought about the case of Hamish McLaren versus his (latest) fifteen victims. He'd stolen $7.66 million over six years, seemed to be motivated by greed, went to great lengths to perform his thievery and didn't just breach trust – he annihilated it. In my opinion, it was likely Hamish was going to be on the extreme end of the sentence for fraud, minus twenty-five per cent for pleading guilty. (But then again, I might have been biased.)

Before heading to the courthouse, Greg and I made a quick detour to meet up with Bec and her boys, Karen and Jane at a cafe. Once well and truly caffeinated and equipped with packs of tissues, we walked into the courthouse arm in arm before taking our seats in the public gallery. Unlike the plea hearing audience, the room was packed with journalists, photographers and families of the victims. Some were already holding back tears while others stood stoically.

A few minutes later, Hamish entered the courtroom, this time wearing a grey suit instead of his prison greens. *How did he even get hold of that suit?* Just like at the hearing when I watched him plead guilty, seeing him look pale and tired (and even more bald) made it easier for me to lay to rest the idea of Max Tavita and accept the reality of Hamish McLaren.

One of the first orders of business was to provide an update on how Hamish had been spending his time in jail. In an attempt to show that he had been displaying 'good behaviour', Hamish's defence spoke of his strong work ethic. Evidently, Hamish was masquerading as a qualified plumber and leading a prison work crew. This bit of information made both Bec and me literally laugh out loud. I'm not joking – the reverberation of our extremely audible response against the courtroom walls caused an uncomfortable number of eyes to land on us.

Here's why Hamish being a plumber is so funny – the man couldn't even lift the lid of a toilet seat with his bare hands because he was such a germaphobe. He also had major neuroses when it came to bowel movements. On the rare occasion he'd need to poo at my apartment, he made me leave the building to grab coffees and croissants for breakfast. Long story short, we did not have the type of relationship where you fart in front of each other. Bec and I had bonded over Hamish's bathroom issues, which is why we laughed at the idea of Hamish working on prison pipes that are packed with the urine and faecal matter of hundreds of men.

Hamish's defence team also attempted to reduce his sentence. They reiterated that he'd pleaded guilty and asked the judge to take into consideration that Hamish was a 'first offender' (pfffft). Thankfully, the judge presiding over the matter, Judge Charteris, rejected the idea that Hamish, who'd literally pleaded guilty to eighteen different charges of fraud from multiple victims, was a first offender. It could have been due to the severity of Hamish's crimes or his lack of remorse, but the judge showed little, if any, compassion for Hamish. Instead of taking the opportunity to personally apologise to his victims in court, Hamish opted to write a letter about how 'truly sorry he was' and that he in fact 'deserved the label of a con man'.

Judge Charteris said that Hamish's letter contained 'a paucity of explanation' and that it didn't persuade him remotely that Hamish was sorry. 'I do not believe he has any remorse. I believe he is consumed by himself ... the one focus was his wellbeing, so he could live, apparently, the high life, while spending the retirement savings of others.'

If the letter didn't help Hamish, Chris's 'character reference' certainly didn't either. Chris was the only family member present and I expected him to give a glowing account of the positive personality traits of Hamish. Unfortunately for Hamish, Chris might not have been the best person to deliver this reference. In response to multiple questions Judge Charteris asked about Hamish, Chris replied that Hamish was generous and liked to spend money, but 'did have a tendency to tell lies'. He said that 'Hamish would watch a James Bond movie and then dress like James Bond. Same suit, same hair.'

Judge Charteris pointed out that Hamish's victims were still owed a total of $5.4 million, or $900,000 a year over the six years of his offending. 'Even James Bond would have trouble spending $900,000 a year,' Judge Charteris said.

This is it. We are so close!

After a solid three hours of the hearing, I think everyone was disappointed when the judge said he needed more time to decide on the sentence. A week, specifically.

A week? Seven days? 168 hours? 10,080 minutes? How would I possibly pass the time?!

Thankfully, motherhood and work kept me occupied, as did daily chats with Bec and Karen. 'Stay strong', 'We're almost there', became our mantras.

Finally, a week later, we were back in a packed courtroom. Hamish, who'd tried to weasel his way out of facing the music by requesting a video conference, was back in the hot seat. Grateful his request had been denied, I kept my eyes glued to him while Judge Charteris spent more than two hours recounting the many ways Hamish McLaren had harmed his fifteen (latest) victims. He detailed our financial losses and emotional devastation before highlighting the long-term impacts that Hamish would no doubt have on all of us.

Judge Charteris said, 'This offender preyed upon the victims. He had the ability to persuade them to part with their money. He had no empathy for them. He was driven by the main game, which was to obtain their money to spend as he wished.' The judge added, 'I've regrettably come to the view that Mr McLaren is not remorseful [and is] sorry for no-one other than himself.'

After making the statement that 'being a con man was not a curable condition', Judge Charteris began handing down his sentence. Even though it was an aggregated sentencing, the judge stated the amount of time Hamish would have served victim by victim. Bec, Karen, Jane, Greg and I were each adding up the years as the judge spoke. Just as we'd hoped, Hamish Earle McLaren was given the maximum sentence (less twenty-five per cent of the time for pleading guilty): sixteen years imprisonment with twelve years non-parole.

As that quite significant puzzle piece soaked into every fibre of my being, everything started to become dark. Thinking I was going to pass out, I steadied myself by placing my hands on the seat in front of me. When I looked around, I could see everyone was clapping but it was as if I had noise-cancelling headphones. The darkness continued to engulf me until I put my head between my knees. *Sixteen years.*

'You can remove Mr McLaren from the court,' Judge Charteris said.

I looked up and saw Hamish, who never once looked back, as he made his exit. Tears began to fall from all his victims, including from the most stoic of stoics. Even though my mind was telling me that I was happy, relieved and grateful, I was at a loss for words when Greg asked me how I was feeling about the outcome. It was a strange feeling to know you have had a role in putting someone in jail. It was not something that was ever on my vision board growing up. I think I managed to say that I was happy with the outcome, but honestly, it was a blur.

Aside from wearing a huge smile, all I could really do was exchange hugs and wipe my face with tissues before walking outside and into a wall of reporters. As I answered question after question about the sentencing, I noticed that a large portion of the shame I had once felt so deeply about being one of Hamish's victims had lifted. There was a sense of pride in being able to say, 'This happened and I survived.' A lot of people consider the word 'victim' to be a bad thing because it implies you were weak, vulnerable, harmed, injured, killed, tricked or duped. I was vulnerable, I was harmed and I was duped. But to be clear – I am a victim of a crime, not a victim of circumstance.

When the media finally trickled away, a group of us went to a pub down the road and shared a few bottles of rosé. Still collectively rallying around each other, we discussed the day, processed and workshopped what we had just witnessed, and knew that this was all part of the healing process.

•

One of the most interesting things that stood out to me during Hamish's sentencing was a comment Judge Charteris made about us victims most likely never seeing our money again. Since the day Hamish was arrested, I had been wondering where our money went. For two years, I was given the same answer from police: 'You'll be given further information about your flow of funds after he's sentenced.' Given that the evidence did not reveal specifically where our money went and that $5.6 million remains unaccounted for, I made a request to the NSW police commissioner on behalf of the victims that further action be taken to explain to us in full where the money went.

Like with most of my experiences trying to get information from the police or justice system, there was a lot of 'kind regards' type correspondence, even more delays and the familiar, 'We are not at liberty to share that information with you' type outcomes. Two years after Hamish's arrest, I still couldn't accept how information like bank records could be 'unknown' or 'not able to be discussed'. In response to my request to the police commissioner, Detective Tom called us into Manly Station to answer the questions we had. To be brutally honest, we did not get any further clarity. We assumed that Hamish had passed money between us to keep his con going. What we didn't know was where he funnelled the missing $5.6 million to because they weren't able to give us that level of detail. Sadly, we still don't have answers.

I can see why people give up when they're in a legal battle. It takes so much energy to keep showing up, keep wondering and keep fighting for what's right. The justice system, as strong as it is, is designed for marathoners, not sprinters. So, while I feel it's worth exploring every avenue to track down where my money could be, I do have a level of acceptance that I may never know. Of course, part of me wants the money back because it was my financial future. But more than that, I just want the rest of the story.

As for Hamish? Well, he wanted to get out early. A year after the sentencing, the world was six months into the Covid-19 pandemic and I was logging onto Zoom to watch my ex-boyfriend appeal the sixteen-year sentence I'd helped achieve. Hamish's defence team argued that the judge had been too harsh on Hamish and more empathetic than necessary with the victims. They also said there wasn't enough weight given to his 'unusual upbringing' and mental health. The appeal document argued that Hamish, who felt like a loner and harboured feelings of abandonment, grew up feeling like he had to earn his father's acceptance by being a high achiever.

Don't we all have family issues? I didn't even know you could use something like this as a defence! I also didn't know just how good of a performer Hamish was until we got to the part in the appeal where his team argued that the judge didn't take Hamish's newfound Christian faith into account when sentencing either. Apparently, he'd been taking bible studies classes through Emmaus Correspondence School and asking meaningful questions at the Sunday service he attended in prison.

Pretty much everyone I've met who's known Hamish in some capacity will attest to the fact that he's a staunch atheist. Unless he's lying about that too. But bible study? Please. As outlandish as these arguments sounded, the judges making the decision must have found merit in them. In early 2021, we were informed that Hamish's sentence was reduced by four years – now twelve years imprisonment, with a non-parole period of nine years, to date from 11 July 2017. That means Hamish will become eligible for parole on 10 July 2026.

Like I said before, Hamish is part of the richness of my life story. Does that mean I'm okay with the fact that he could potentially be walking free in 2026? No. Does that mean I dwell on what happened day and night? No. But I will tell you this – not a day has passed in the last six years that I haven't thought about what happened in some way. In the early years, the daily thoughts were about what he did, how he did it, what I lost, how devastated I'd felt, and how ashamed and anxious I became. As time went by, the ruminating stopped but I still feel fleeting aftershocks of the pain he inflicted or find myself remembering another little detail of his deceptions. Nowadays, I find myself being more reflective with my perspective. I even manage a few laughs along the way.

It may never happen, but it would be nice to wake up one day and have the realisation, '*Wow, I didn't think about Hamish yesterday!*' Until then, the healing work continues.

CHAPTER 30

But Why Did He Do It?

It's not lost on me how big, fanciful, ridiculous and sometimes truly unbelievable the stories 'Max Tavita' told me might seem … especially when they are extracted from the rest of our mundane conversations and printed on a piece of paper or turned into a soundbite. What's difficult to convey with two-dimensional typed words or ten seconds of airtime are the subtleties and nuances of how the stories were told to me. Delivered at the right moments and in an appropriate tone, Max's stories came out in bits and pieces, a sentence at a time, almost feeling like the minutiae of our relationship. While a few things he said were outlandish or arrogant, there was nothing so glaring that I had to question, 'Hang on, is that what *really* happened, Max?' So yes, there were some grey areas but at the time, everything added up. Until it didn't.

I needed to understand how Hamish had been able to chameleon his way into being the type of man I could love and the type of man to whom victims would give a reported estimate of $80 to $100 million. I decided to pop on my armchair-FBI criminal profiler hat and get to work dissecting the con artist that is Hamish McLaren. Full disclosure: I am not a trained psychiatrist or psychologist. Aside from listening to copious amounts of true crime podcasts, I have no experience in criminal justice. I am also in no way even attempting to be objective when sharing my following (very personal) views on the psyche of my least favourite person. Alright, let's get started.

Trait #1: Might be a psychopath
One of the things that shook me the most about Hamish was how soundly he could sleep beside me while simultaneously stealing my life savings behind my back. While I won't say for certain he wasn't faking it because, come on, I was lying next to one of the world's most prolific con men, I will say that the rhythm of his breathing and sporadic hypnic jerks were very convincing. Meanwhile, I was usually battling restless leg syndrome, counting sheep, stressing about something I'd said in 1996 and wondering if melatonin could be injected intravenously. In hindsight, I should have been counting all the ways I might be being duped by the man who held my hand late into the evening, rubbed magnesium on my legs and cocooned me if I was having a rough day. The fact that Hamish could sleep at night while knowingly robbing from someone he 'loved' (along with a raft of other unsuspecting victims) led me to conclude that he must be a sociopath.

However, when I looked up the definition of 'sociopath', it didn't fit. Hamish went out of his way to make it seem like he cared about me, always appeared calm and even-keeled and wasn't acting hot-headed or impulsive. Next, I looked up 'psychopath' and read that it's used to describe someone who has relationships that are shallow and fake, fails to form genuine emotional attachments and (wait for it) maintains a normal life to cover up criminal activity. It might not be a formal diagnosis, but it certainly makes me feel comfortable calling Hamish a psychopath.

Trait #2: Weaponises empathy
By definition, empathy means 'the ability to understand, imagine and share the feelings and emotions of another'. Upon retracing my steps as well as speaking with his other victims, I realised that Hamish was able to communicate in a way that made you feel like he was the ultimate empath. However, instead of using his empathy superpowers of understanding another person's feelings for good, he weaponised them to uncover his victim's vulnerabilities so he knew where and when to strike.

Chris Voss, a former FBI hostage negotiator and author, writes in *Never Split the Difference* about a concept called 'tactical empathy'. This strategy can be used to uncover everything you need to know about what is driving a person as well as what's holding them back. Hamish's greatest strength was engaging someone in conversation, listening like a bat and then getting tactical with his empathy. It didn't matter if we were discussing future dreams or unpacking childhood trauma, it was as if Hamish truly 'understood' and 'empathised'.

Hamish didn't just hold eye contact, nod his head or mirror body language when listening. He had thoughtful follow-up questions, rarely pontificated (I say rarely because he did have strong opinions about us living in a matrix) and always offered the response I needed. Sometimes that was wisdom, sometimes it was a reminder to reframe my thinking and other times it was a solid ego-stroking session to help get the wind back in my sails. Regardless of the words coming out of his mouth, his energy always matched what I needed too. He could exude 'strong and decisive' just as easily as he could 'tender, compassionate and (you guessed it) empathetic'.

When the roles were reversed and I was the one actively listening, Hamish shared just enough of his own tragedies, pain and secrets that I felt safe to open up about my own. Clever guy. What did Hamish do with the information he uncovered? In my case, he used it to become the type of man I'd said I was looking for because he knew I'd trust this man. He knew I'd fall in love. Early on in our relationship, 'Max Tavita' uncovered all the things I wanted from a potential partner. I wanted someone with a solid moral compass and strong family values, who didn't abuse drugs or alcohol, was reliable and respectful, was happy to stay in and chill on a Saturday night from time to time and who valued their health and relationships above all. Basically, through our many deep conversations, I painted a picture of the person I wanted in my life, which meant all Hamish had to do was listen and then create Max to be that.

Sure, I got to see Hamish's OG 'high-flying investment banker' persona through his 'work'. But for the majority of our time together, he actively portrayed himself as the new, down-to-earth 'I just want a simple life' Max. For how dramatic dating a con man sounds, it actually felt like a pretty stock standard mid-forties relationship. As well as the lacklustre sex, we weren't hitting the town and we weren't hopping on yachts. We just lived in *my* happy place – staying in for the night and spending our free days at the beach enjoying the surf, sunshine, saltwater and sandy feet.

Trait #3: Has attachment issues

Even though Hamish was Max when we were together, you'll recall that I was always either 'TT', 'T', 'Rascal' or 'Bub' and Asha was 'Jerry'. Even Gracie the cat was 'The Rat'. As I sit here literally scratching my head, I can't help but wonder what that was about. Was it the Aussie in him? Or was it subconsciously so he didn't have to get close to the real us? Even if it wasn't about detaching from his victims, I'm not surprised that Hamish had to make up some fake family fantasy.

Remember how he told me his parents died in a plane crash when he was six? Well, thanks to Greg's reporting for *Who the Hell is Hamish?*, I learned that Hamish evidently told this story to multiple people, including ex-girlfriends. The location of where and how the plane went down changed but the ending was always the same: Hamish survived, only to be sent to live in foster care or with a terribly neglectful aunty and uncle. He also told an ex-girlfriend a detailed story of how his family was placed in a witness protection program after his mother played a key role in sending a criminal to jail. In an act of rebellion, he and his twin brother, Phil, took off in the car one night with Hamish at the wheel. Three days later, he woke up in a hospital to discover that he'd crashed and Phil was dead. Turns out, Hamish never had a twin, but his dad's name is Phil.

When I think about it, it's as if Hamish was always trying to create a life more interesting than his own. Was he trying to impress his parents? Did he not feel like he lived up to expectations? His appeal defence seemed to believe this to be true. One day when we were dating, Hamish said he was on his way up to Avalon to drop off a birthday card for his aunty or uncle. I still don't know whether this was all just a load of shit or if he went up to see his parents, who we now know are very much alive and well and living in Avalon. Apparently, he tried to reconnect with them after a long hiatus in 2016, so it could be (kind of) true.

Trait #4: 'Lies low' due to past criminal activity
In episode 7 of *Who the Hell is Hamish?*, Greg shared that Hamish had grown up in Avalon and attended Pittwater House school. While some people who knew Hamish and his family agreed that his parents weren't the type to give warm shows of affection, they also agreed that Hamish aka 'Hambone' was a total legend. Funny, outgoing, genuine, loyal and a passionate surfer are just a few of the ways people described him. When I think about how popular Hamish had been on the Northern Beaches as a teen, coupled with the publicity he had gained in the early 2000s from failing in the futures market and stealing $5 million

from Harts Australasia investors, it makes perfect sense why he was so keen for 'nights in' and 'living the simple life' in faraway Canada, the UK and, more recently, Bondi.

Hamish's need to avoid people explains why he was so happy to adopt my low-key lifestyle. His need for 'Max' to not get caught explains why he went to great lengths to keep me from meeting his family, colleagues and friends. But what I don't have an explanation for (yet) is who the other characters were in the Max Tavita Show. Throughout our relationship, I heard Max on the phone or via video conference on numerous occasions. There was always a real person on the other end. I could hear them, see them and sometimes even interact with them myself. Let's take Ana, for example. Not only did I watch them communicate via phone or video on a weekly basis, I actually met her in person.

About a year into our relationship, Hamish was having dinner with Ana Terrén and another person at The Apollo in Potts Point. I had been working late but caught an Uber to meet up with Max. When I arrived, there were brief introductions before Max strongly suggested we go have a drink in Bondi and head home. Happy to have an early one, we hopped in a cab back to Max's apartment. Max relayed that Ana had texted that we should have stayed for a drink. When I said I totally would have, he made the cute comment that he just wanted me all to himself. This was another example where no names were used … other than me introducing myself as Tracy.

Then there was the 'Foster Fam'. In the version I heard, this foster family took Max in after a series of bad placements. Hamish spoke about this family a lot; their names, their kids' names, wives' names, the name of the company they owned, the parents who he considered his own parents. I heard countless conversations on the phone between Max and the three boys and their father. In my mind, and in this fake world he created, they were his family and he was the fourth son.

Funny story – in early 2016, a friend of mine was at the fortieth birthday of the wife of one of the 'Foster Fam' boys when she ran into Hamish. Given my friend had been friends with Hamish's niece and had spent a substantial amount of time with Hamish during his days in Curl Curl, she laughed in his face when he introduced himself as 'Max'. Her response: 'Fuck off, Hamish, it's Kate.' To which he replied: 'Oh, yeah, yeah, hi.' This exchange makes me think Hamish was in the process of constructing 'Max' but couldn't get too far with it on the Northern Beaches since he knew too many people.

Trait #5: Knows when to enlist the help of others

On another occasion, I heard Max having a conversation with Bec's dad. They were talking about 'the boys he missed so much'. Today, I've fact-checked this and can tell you that whoever he was speaking with was not Bec's dad. So who was it? I'm not sure. However, it makes me wonder if Hamish had people in the background on standby waiting for him to call so they could fake a conversation for him. It also makes me wonder if he had people working *with* him. Over the course of our relationship, I met or heard the voices of friends and colleagues. Were any of them in on it? Or were they just additional pawns in his game of chess?

Trait #6: Calculated and manipulative

Whether it was intentional or not, I can see that the roles Hamish created were one of the key ways that he was grooming me to trust him with my life savings. Without hearing him and others speak with such confidence and frequency about finance and investing, I'm not sure I would have had the faith in him that I did. On top of having cast members (who may well not have known what Hamish was up to), Hamish made solid use of props. Every Friday, he wrote and delivered a detailed report for his 'family office investors'. Packed full of pie charts, line graphs and pages of facts, figures and projections, it led me to believe that Hamish really knew what he was talking about. He'd forward me a copy of the email almost weekly with just 'FYI' in the subject line. Other props included the letters I collected from his letterbox addressed to *Max Tavita*, the falsified investment statements on Bell Potter letterhead, the forms I filled out and had witnessed that were never lodged, pictures of his apartment in NYC, pictures of the Aston Martin he owned and that was in one of his garage parking spots, as well as the 'for sale' apartments he FaceTimed me from.

Trait #7: Motivated by greed (or sick thrills)

As it started to become clearer how Hamish did what he did, I began to wonder why. Was it just to earn as much money as he could? Was it to create a life that was far more exciting and grandiose than his own? Was it because he genuinely had a hard-on for Swiss watches, private jets and houses with so much square footage they required a name?

According to criminologist Donald R Cressey's 'Fraud Triangle' theory, there are three contributing factors that compel someone to commit fraud: motivation, opportunity and rationalisation. At first, I think Hamish was motivated by greed. He didn't just want money to get by, he wanted it so that he could buy (these are his words) 'look back' luxury cars. A past connection of Hamish's asked him about why he referred to his Porsche as a 'look back' car. He replied, 'Because every time I park and walk away, I look back and think – I own that!' Over time, I think his Ponzi scheme grew so large that he became motivated by the need to get more funds to keep 'investors' from getting suspicious. I also often wonder if it was some kind of sick game. Who, how and what can I take next? – that type of thing. Did he get some sort of perverse thrill from having someone believe a lie or hand over their money? Maybe.

Trait #8: Can't stop, won't stop

As for opportunity and rationalisation ... From what I've been able to find, it looks like Hamish's greed and crimes began on Sydney's Futures Exchange trading floor. Actually, it began shortly after high school when he went on a ski trip to Canada with his friends who'd just finished Year 12. While in Canada, he met a man who helped him go from a Northern Beaches landscape labourer to Sydney trader. Unfortunately for Hamish (and all of his victims), he sucked at it, which is what ultimately paved the way for him to start swindling people out of their money.

By the time Hamish had gotten to me, he was running a fully fledged Ponzi scheme. But well before he was faking investment reports on a Friday afternoon, he was convincing a couple he knew from his days on the trading floors to go in on a 'business deal' with him to import fish from Tonga. In the early 90s, the husband of the couple had recently received a redundancy payout and was looking for an opportunity to invest. Hamish may not have known how to spot a real investment, but man was he good at spotting an opportunity for a fake one. The couple says that Hamish made them feel confident that he knew what he was talking about. If anything, it was like Hamish was making them prove their knowledge and commitment to the deal. Eventually, they put up all the money for the business as well as a car. Within days, the money, the car and Hamish were long gone. When police finally tracked down the car, it was abandoned with a wad of parking tickets under the wiper blade.

By the time Greg reached the end of his investigation for *Who the Hell is Hamish?*, he'd discovered that the Royal Canadian Mounted Police had warrants for Hamish's arrest and he was under investigation in Hong Kong. And long before ASIC had slapped a ban on him and he'd been bankrupted, a letter had been sent to the NSW Crime Squad with a dossier of evidence. In the letter, the author stated that they had strong reason to believe that Hamish Watson was responsible for fraudulently acquiring investment funds from companies and individuals in excess of $20 million.

'My family alone were defrauded of around $7 million over a 3–4 year period,' the author of the letter wrote.

With so many people sniffing him out, it makes a lot of us think that Hamish could have been stopped much sooner than he was. The 'system' failed for three decades until two young detectives from Manly came along. While I genuinely hope that I get to remain Hamish's last victim, I am a realist and fear that it's not going to be the case. Detectives have already allegedly intercepted financial crimes that Hamish has attempted to orchestrate from jail. Greed is a powerful motivator but it's hard for me to think that's the full story. Like the saying goes, 'Hurt people hurt people'.

CHAPTER 31

Who the Hell is Tracy?

Thanks to Google, Greg, my fellow Hamish Club members and notes from Hamish's psychiatric evaluations, I now know very well who Hamish is. He's someone with a long-standing pattern of inherent maladaptive personality traits who uses dishonesty and manipulation for personal gain. Purely driven by greed, his callous disregard for victims enabled him to hurt me and many others to the magnitude that he did. A true outlier, I personally feel like the only thing Hamish can boast about is being in the top 0.1% of psychopathic offenders. (It's not Mensa but it's something!) In a nutshell: he is, on some sick level, a genius who also happens to be a word that would have my grandmother rolling over in her grave if I used it.

When I was approaching the two-year anniversary of Hamish's arrest, I realised that there was one post-Max question in particular that needed to be answered. *Who the hell is Tracy?* On paper, I was someone with a long-standing pattern of believing everyone was inherently good and who uses her positivity bias for pretty much all decision-making. Predominantly driven by love, my propensity to trust enabled Hamish to hurt me and other kind people to the extent that he did. Sounds like a pretty decent and well-meaning chick, right? In a world of only rainbows and sunshine, she would *thrive*. But that's not the case, is it?

As part of my self-discovery journey, I took the time I used to dedicate to sleuthing and stressing over Hamish's sentencing to get back to doing the things that had once brought me joy. Here's the thing about trauma – it is the thief of joy. Often masquerading as anxiety, it can and will hold you back from loving fully, opening up completely and enjoying your happiness. Knowing I didn't want Hamish to rob me of even more, I started volunteering as a mentor to teenage girls, became a board member of a men's mental health charity, started playing competitive soccer after a twenty-year hiatus and thoughtfully penned a '50 Before 50' list that included goals like 'Run a Marathon', 'Take Asha to Nepal' and 'Coach Young Marketers'.

Most crucially, I continued to invest in my emotional growth by doing therapy, EMDR, breathwork, sleep therapy, float tanks, travel and massage. Given I'm pretty contained emotionally, I know that the trauma has built up in my body and I am determined not to let it take over my sleep, mind or body. I know that some of this could be considered a bit witchy woo woo, but it's all part of the exploration and I never want to stop exploring and growing in this space. Take what works, leave what doesn't.

Through my healing work, I found myself looking back on my dating history and realised that my two most significant relationships ended in divorce or jail time. It was hard for me not to think, *Why do I choose these people?* How was it that I could launch the world's first virtual reality department store where you shop with your eyes – yet I couldn't see the monster in front of me?

In the case of Hamish, I chose Max because he quickly became exactly who I had pictured for Act II of 'Tracy's Life'. Today, I know it's because Hamish callously created him to be just that. There's a good chance I also chose Max because compared to the other options on Happn, Max looked like George Clooney on the cover of *Sports Illustrated*. Not really – he wasn't the hottest guy around but he 'got' me with his sense of humour and values and I felt seen. And finally, there's the chance I chose him because I was vulnerable. Anxious to gain clarity around what it was about me that made Hamish pounce, I took 'Why do I choose these people?' along with an additional question, 'What is it about me that attracts these situations into my life?' to my therapist.

When Bertie answered, she did not hold back. 'Tracy? Really? You think this is your issue? Your personality malfunction? To me this is a form of victim blaming. It's like you're trying to say it's you who has the personality defect.' She then reminded me that vulnerability is not a bad thing. We are all vulnerable at different points in life. The reality is, Bertie emphasised, that I met someone (arguably a psychopath) who took advantage of me when I was in a vulnerable state. 'It's not *you*. It's him. You didn't *attract* Hamish. You were simply unlucky enough to meet the wrong guy at the wrong time. It could have happened to anyone.'

Someone recently asked me when I first experienced 'victim blaming' in relation to my experiences with Hamish. The truth is – it happened almost instantly and it was from myself. In the cesspit of my sorrow in the months following Hamish's arrest, I was the one questioning how I could have let this happen. While my therapist's words certainly helped me in the self-compassion department, they mostly got me thinking about vulnerability and trust. In the first year after I left my ex-husband, I was running on huge amounts of adrenaline in pretty much every life area. As a result, when I started dating, I was still hyper-focused on ticking off my life-admin to-do list while working full-time and single parenting. While most people think of emotions or self-esteem when they think of vulnerability, I'm here to remind you that vulnerability comes in many different forms. I wasn't vulnerable because I was desperate to feel loved or validated. I was vulnerable because I was distracted. I was vulnerable because I was tired. I was also vulnerable because it's in our nature to trust. And I did want a connection.

When Hamish went fishing for his next victim online in 2016, I fully believe he was looking for a catch that came with a career and salary. After successfully 'hooking' me, he did what any psychopath with the goal of stealing all your money would do: he strategically gained my trust. It's safe to say that Hamish deeply understood the psychology of trust and used it against me. By taking the time to ask me questions and actively listen, he discovered that I wasn't impressed with multi-million-dollar homes, luxury cars and celebrity name-dropping. Then he shapeshifted into the trustworthy man I'd dreamed up for my second act. The cars went into the background, the 'generational wealth' chat dialled down and within weeks, he was just a simple laidback guy who loved the ocean, running and hearing me talk about hot chips with chicken salt.

As I write this six years after Hamish's arrest, I tread a delicate line between self-blame and acceptance. I still hear my mind whisper, 'You should have known', from time to time. When this voice chimes in, it's important for me to remember that Hamish was a professional who had honed his craft for over twenty years. With decades of experience in the art of deceit and having his con be his full-time job, his actions were subtle. So subtle that I, the too-busy-to-look-for-every-red-fucking-flag single working mum, didn't notice them. Hamish truly was phenomenal at his job, which is why aside from me, most of his victims came to him via word of mouth and genuine recommendations. It's also important for me to remember that there were many more extremely intelligent, successful and 'savvy businesspeople' who were conned by Hamish. Just because you're successful and intelligent doesn't mean you're not vulnerable.

When the judge gave his final statement at Hamish's sentencing, I'll never forget him saying, 'Hamish preyed on the vulnerability of these people as if it was their problem. The human condition is inherently vulnerable.' Everyone is going to be vulnerable at different points in your life.

If not, you're not living in the realm of humanity. So, while yes, vulnerability played a part in making me a victim of Hamish McLaren, it's also what makes me human.

I could see many reasons why I had chosen Australia's Mr Ripley and could see that none of it was my fault, but even so, I still wasn't sure how I was going to feel whole and confident enough to trust someone again, let alone myself. My straight-shooting therapist weighed in at my next session.

'I don't think you see yourself how others see you.'

'What do you mean?' I asked.

'I mean, I question whether you see yourself as intelligent, beautiful and as worthy of love as you actually are.'

This compliment made me immediately uncomfortable and I launched into a light-hearted self-deprecating defence.

'Let me put it this way,' Bertie explained. 'You're a ten and you're dating threes. Maybe not in looks and superficial charm department, but as humans, they're a three. You need to raise the bar.'

I walked out of Bertie's office thinking about how uncomfortable it felt to hear this. Was it Tall Poppy Syndrome? My fear of the spotlight? Self-doubt? Why didn't I want to fully believe that I was intelligent, beautiful and worthy of love? Clearly, I still had some work to do. While I'm sure my inner child (and inner twenty-something) needed to be hugged, I found myself journaling all the truths I knew.

Truth: You cannot grieve if you cannot love.
Truth: I love love.

Truth: Shame can only survive in the dark.
Truth: I will always search for the light.
Truth: Red flags are just flags when you look at the world
through rose-coloured glasses.
Truth: My positivity bias may have resulted in poor decisions,
but it's also what helped me survive.
Truth: Being vulnerable isn't a bad thing.
Truth: You have to sit with the hard stuff and let yourself feel it all.
Truth: Showing self-compassion is not a set and forget deal.
Truth: Being resilient isn't about strength, it's about adaptability.

There was a life before Hamish. A big life full of great things and crap things. There has been a life after Hamish and hopefully it will continue for another fifty or so years. In the ultimate scheme of things, Hamish was a blip on my life journey but a blip that has caused me to reconsider and re-evaluate all I know and believe to be true. What's interesting is that while I've blamed myself for things happening, I've never questioned whatever higher power is out there, 'Why me?' or 'Why have all these things happened to me?' It's taken work, but I've always accepted that good things happen to bad people and bad things happen to good people. But I can't lie, there have been many moments when I've thought 'I'm not sure I can handle this' or 'I can't take anymore'. People who are conned or in a psychologically manipulative relationship have to show themselves a huge amount of self-compassion because, vulnerable or not, you can't know until you know.

Before Hamish, if you'd asked me what it meant to be resilient, I would have said it was all about standing your ground and weathering every storm that life throws at you. When Dad died, my marriage fell apart and Mum got sick, I did whatever I could to stand strong and stand tall. But after Hamish, I realised that resilience is also about adaptability. In the same way a tree lets its branches blow with the wind, acceptance of the storm can often be the more forgiving path.

CHAPTER 32

Rethinking Trust

As utterly horrific as my experience has been, I'm grateful for it, which begs a question I feel like indulging. Do I regret creating a dating app profile at the end of 2015?

No, I honestly don't regret it.

While I certainly wish I could have figured out that Hamish was not to be trusted well before I lost my life savings, I don't even regret that I dated him. I've thought a lot about what advice I'll give Asha and her friends when they paddle into the dating pool that will no doubt be filled with a few floating Band-Aids. This may come as a shock, but it's not 'stay off the dating apps!', 'get 100 points of identification' and 'be highly attuned to the red flags!' Why? Because that's a shitty existence.

If you enter a relationship looking for reasons to doubt it, you're going to become cynical, closed off and too scared to take the risks necessary to build a connection and cultivate love. Like it or not, you cannot love if you cannot trust.

The key is knowing *how* to trust, which is why my first piece of advice will be to read the following books:

- *Thinking, Fast and Slow* by Daniel Kahneman
- *The Confidence Game* by Maria Konnikova
- *The Power of Vulnerability* by Brené Brown

My second piece of advice would be to become aware of any potential cognitive biases that may be in play, such as confirmation bias. Professor Roderick M Kramer wrote the article 'Rethinking Trust' in the June 2009 edition of the *Harvard Business Review*. In it, Kramer argues that social stereotypes heavily influence us to conclude that someone is honest, reliable and trustworthy based on their gender, age, race, facial expressions, socioeconomic status, employer's reputation, and/or the fact that they run in the same social circle as you. Most of the time, there's not a huge amount of harm in this type of subconscious judgement. It's when our confirmation bias causes us to overestimate a person's trustworthiness that we run into trouble.

My third piece of advice would be: take time (even sleep on it!) to think critically about the person or opportunity in front of you. While I can see how my similarities to Hamish, historical outcomes and post-rationalisations influenced the trust I extended to Hamish, it's critical thinking that I could have been far better at. To be clear, I don't think I could have critically thought my way into believing that the man who was spooning me at night was plotting to take all my money. Hamish was a master when it came to making me feel secure, strong and like I had every reason in the world to trust that he had my best interests at heart. What I mean is that I could have thought far more critically about the investment opportunities he was presenting to me. Just like I trusted my lawyer to handle my divorce, I trusted Hamish to handle my superannuation. If I had dug just that little bit deeper when 'Max' had told me he was 'privy to information' in the US stock market, I would have found a whole lot of reasons to start questioning my trust.

As for my last two pieces of advice? Don't be afraid to get it wrong and give yourself time to heal. It's unrealistic to think you're going to walk through life getting everything right. Also – who would want to? It's usually our farts, failures and fuckups that teach us the real lessons we need to live a life that is authentic, meaningful and purposeful. These lessons can only be learned when we give ourselves time to sit with our emotions, reflect and rebuild. It may seem counterintuitive to embrace our lowest of lows, but as Glennon Doyle writes in *Untamed*, 'First the pain, then the waiting, then the rising.' So while I want Asha to rethink how society has conditioned us to intrinsically trust, I mostly want her to focus on learning how to trust the person who matters most: herself. I want her to trust that she will inevitably 'get it wrong' from time to time and that it's absolutely okay. It took a solid five years for me to finally be able to view what happened between Hamish and me with grace, perspective and love. And full disclosure – the healing is still happening.

From early on, I knew I wanted to write about this experience, but I can see now just how painful and one-sided it could have been if I hadn't been able to wait for the rising. I remember reading an Instagram post by Glennon Doyle that shared Nadia Bolz-Weber's widsom. 'If you're going to share widely, make sure you're sharing from your scars, not your open wounds.' My experiences have made me who I am, but they don't define me. You have no idea how grateful I am to be able to wholeheartedly say that I wrote this book from a scar and not an open wound. I am no longer ashamed of my history and proud to talk about it. In return, I'd love for people to share their stories with me. Like shame, most wounds dry out beautifully in the sunlight.

Epilogue

In 2022 alone, Australians reported a total combined loss of $3.1 billion to targeting scams. Of that figure, $1.5 billion was lost to investment scams, $229 million to remote access scams and $224 million to payment redirection scams. Seeing as thirty per cent of victims don't report scams to anyone, the actual losses are estimated to be far higher. If this information is as mind-boggling to you as it is to me, then please keep this conversation going. By talking about stories like mine, we can make it harder for people like Hamish McLaren to operate in society. And even more importantly, we can help break the stigma about reporting scams.

Every other week, another piece of information comes that adds colour and context to this story. And every other week, I'm reminded of just how crucial it is that women in particular are financially literate, financially empowered and, most importantly, financially independent. It's not lost on me how much of a privilege it was that I had a full-time job to keep me afloat when Hamish wiped out my savings. This is just one of the many reasons why I now spend much of my time writing and speaking publicly about financial independence, romance scams and our need to normalise situational vulnerability. Of all the questions I've been trying to answer while writing this book, I'm sure there's one you're dying to know: any news about where the money went?

No.

I'd love to be able to add a 'not yet' after that full stop, but the more I look into white-collar crimes, the more I accept the reality that my money is long gone. The police can't help any further, the courts won't help and the banks definitely won't help. My money could be sitting in an offshore account waiting for Hamish or it could have been used to pacify another victim we don't even know about. Or he could have gambled it away on the pokies at his local RSL.

Either way, I don't like to indulge thoughts like 'What if I didn't lose my life savings?' or 'Maybe I'll get my money back'. When I start playing the 'what if and maybe' game, I feel like a victim who has her eyes wide and hands out waiting for someone else to make everything okay again. To hold out hope for something that is completely out of my control feels like admitting defeat in a way. It feels more helpful to focus on what I do have. Hamish stole my money and the future I *thought* I would have, but he did not steal my right, ability and determination to drive my own outcomes.

Like I said before, I am a victim of a crime but not a victim of circumstance. It's taken a whole lot of therapy, support from friends and family, a massive mindset shift and a hefty amount of time in the ocean, but I'm beyond proud to be able to write that I have reclaimed and rebuilt my sense of financial independence, learned to operate with scepticism, not cynicism, formed an even tighter bond with Asha and found a strength within me I could never have imagined. Is everything perfect and fail-safe? No way. Sometimes, life still makes me feel off-kilter. But for now, I know that I have everything I need to surf the highs and lows.

At the time this book went to print, I still hadn't watched *The Matrix*.

ACKNOWLEDGEMENTS

Writing *The Last Victim* has been a journey of emotions, challenges, and self-discovery, and I owe a debt of gratitude to those who stood by me. This book is not just a solitary effort but a collective result of love, support and inspiration from incredible individuals who have shaped my life in profound ways.

To Summer Land, my co-author and collaborator. I never could have imagined that our chance meeting at the 2022 Gidget Foundation luncheon would lead to near daily conversations and countless hours of us laughing, crying, ranting and raving as we found a way to make the story I wanted to tell infinitely more interesting and entertaining. On top of your intense curiosity, compassion, and insane storytelling skills, you have a way of helping me see myself in ways I never had before. Thank you for everything.

To the team at Hachette: Sophie, Annie, Cosi and Eliza (plus everyone else behind the scenes I didn't get to meet). Your guidance and support has been insightful and so appreciated. This book is beyond my wildest expectations because of your input, expertise, time and care.

To my agent, Jeanne Ryckmans. You believed in me and championed my reasons for sharing my story from the moment we connected. Thank you for guiding me through the wild and wonderful world of book publishing.

To my marketing family both here and internationally. Your support and gifted resources have been a godsend. I can't tell you how many 'how can I help?' messages I have received ... many of which brought me to tears and reminded me that the universe is totally rigged in my favour. Can also confirm that human cheerleaders provide the best dopamine ever. A special shout out to Mickey Mac who has continuously pumped my tyres and provided so much time and expertise helping this story and book reach as many women as possible.

To my beautiful friends who have listened to me, held me, laughed and cried with me over the years. There are no guidebooks for situations like this, no manual with step-by-step instructions on what to say, how to help, or what to do next. You all stood beside me, walked with me, handed me some sort of food or drink, got me out of the house and held me up when I was falling down. I can't thank you enough and will be eternally grateful for your support and presence in my life.

To Greg Bearup, the man who helped the world find answers for *Who the Hell is Hamish?* This story may never have seen the light of day if it wasn't for you. From the moment we met at a cafe to discuss such a deeply personal experience, you've shown me nothing but respect and compassion. The dedication and work you put towards uncovering the truth about Hamish was instrumental in my healing journey and I will be forever grateful. P.S. I love the random messages I still get from you checking in on me – you're a legend.

To my fellow victims, Bec, Karen, Lorraine, Peter, Glen, Jane, Lisa, Nicole and Julie (and the countless others who were not named and who I've never met). To know I wasn't alone was a blessing. To Bec in particular, thank you for all the laughs and confirmation that I wasn't going crazy at a time when the puzzle was still very jumbled. You are a shining light and deserve all the love in the world.

To Cath, my supersleuth, friend and fierce protector. Thank you for taking the story to Greg, for asking me the tough questions, and for never making me feel stupid for the situation I found myself in. Everyone needs a Cath in their life, but I am not keen to share you with too many more people.

To my brothers, Mikey and Marty. Thank you for keeping me grounded and reminding me that being the middle child (and only girl) toughened me up for life – in a good way.

To the two sisters I've chosen for myself in this life, Cobie and Jaala. Thank you for being the first to read the manuscript and for providing encouragement and wisdom. You have been through my greatest triumphs and stood by me in my deepest sorrows – never wavering, always loving. What would I do without you both?

To Mum, the strongest and most resilient woman I know. Thank you for your unwavering support, the countless sacrifices you have made over the course of your life for me, and for the rational voice of reason I have on autoplay in my head when times get tough. Your strength has been my inspiration and you have taught me the true meaning of perseverance.

To my spirit in the sky, Dad. Thank you for exposing me to all those freaky books on the top shelf, for the security you gave our family, for loving Mum like the queen she is and for always making us laugh in your red undies! Your wisdom and humour echoes in my mind almost every day, and while you are not physically present, you are constantly in my thoughts and in my heart.

To Asha, my hope and reason for getting up every morning when I didn't think I could. You provide me with constant inspiration and belly laughs. Life with you is pure joy, adventure, and insight. I hope you always shine your light as brightly as you do right now. The world needs all the sparkles it can get. I'm so grateful you chose me to be your Mumma.

To Tim, my longtime friend who asked me after Hamish was arrested, 'Do you ever think you'll be able to love again?' At the time, I honestly didn't know. Turns out – it was a huge yes. I'm beyond grateful to be able to write that you are the person who showed me I would love *and trust* again. You gave me strength when I didn't think I had any left and your patience and understanding continues to lift me up in ways I didn't know was possible. It's quite possible that you are my biggest fan, and I, yours. Your belief in me during moments of self-doubt has been so appreciated. One million thank yous.

And finally – thank you to the Universe for providing all the opportunities, adventures, lessons, heartaches and experiences I needed to arrive at this point. There are no accidents and while I have not always understood why, I infinitely trust (and am grateful for) the order of life.

Tracy Hall is an author, keynote speaker and senior marketing executive. Over the last twenty-five years, Tracy has had extensive exposure to start-ups, large corporations and global tech brands including Virgin Mobile, eBay, GoDaddy and Afterpay. She frequently consults for smaller companies, volunteers as a teen mentor for the Raise Foundation and is a board director for the men's mental health charity, Mongrels Men.

In 2019, Tracy became known as Hamish McLaren's famous 'last victim' thanks to her role in *The Australian*'s podcast, *Who the Hell is Hamish?* Today, Tracy writes and speaks publicly about financial empowerment, intimate fraud, and the shame that often comes with being a victim of a scam. Tracy is also passionate about discussing situational vulnerability, the true meaning of resilience and society's need to rethink how we trust.

The Last Victim is her first book.

tracyhall.com.au
tracyleehall

Summer Land is an author, writer, keynote speaker and one-time nude model for a figure drawing class. Born in West Virginia and raised in Florida, Summer graduated magna cum laude from Emerson College (Boston, MA) in 2008 where she studied marketing. After embarking on a working holiday in Australia and spending two ski seasons in Park City, Utah, Summer moved to Australia in 2010 and began writing. Summer's first book, *Summerlandish: Do as I Say, Not as I Did*, was published in 2013 and garnered praise from 2014 Stella Prize winner, Clare Wright, who wrote, 'Summer Land is Gen Y's answer to Bill Bryson.' Her second book, *I Now Pronounce You Husband and Expat*, was published in 2019. Summer has also co-authored and ghostwritten over ten books, including *Acting Up* (Lynne McGranger), *A Joyful Life* (Rosemary Kariuki), and *Aussie Ark* (Tim Faulkner). Known for her sharp wit, intense curiosity and deeply empathetic nature, Summer is passionate about helping tell stories that inspire a more connected, compassionate and creative world.

summerland.me
summerlandwrites

If you would like to find out more about Hachette Australia,
our authors, upcoming events and new releases you can visit
our website or our social media channels:

hachette.com.au

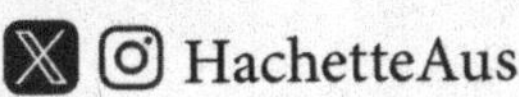 HachetteAustralia

HachetteAus